940.531503
K82v
120158

DATE DUE

WITHDRAWN
L. R. COLLEGE LIBRARY

STATEMENT OF PURPOSE

The *Holocaust Library* was created and is managed by survivors. Its purpose is to offer to the reading public authentic material, not readily available, and to preserve the memory of our martyrs and heroes untainted by arbitrary or inadvertent distortions.

With each passing day the memory of the tragedy of European Jews, the greatest crime in the annals of mankind, recedes into history. The witnesses and survivors of the Holocaust are still alive, their memories remain vivid; yet, a malicious myth about their experience keeps rising before our eyes, distorting and mis- interpreting evidence, perverting history.

As new generations arise, so grows the incredible ignorance about our tragedy. Millions of men and women, Jews and Gen- tiles, are unaware of the basic facts of the tragedy; many have never even heard the word "Holocaust." This is a seed of a new disaster.

The Holocaust story should be untiringly told and retold making the world aware of its lessons. This can contribute to that moral reconstruction which alone may prevent a repetition of the catas- trophe in our hate- and violence-stricken world.

ADVISORY BOARD: Alexander Donat (*Chairman*),
Sam E. Bloch, William H. Donat,
Abraham H. Foxman, Hadassah Rosensaft,
Leon W. Wells, Elie Wiesel

A VOICE
FROM THE FOREST

Memoirs of a Jewish Partisan

by
Nahum Kohn
and
Howard Roiter

CARL A. RUDISILL LIBRARY
LENOIR RHYNE COLLEGE

HOLOCAUST LIBRARY
NEW YORK

940.531503
K82v
120158
Jan. 1982

D
810
.J4
K653
July 2021

Copyright © 1980 by Nahum Kohn and Howard Roiter
Printed in the United States of America

Library of Congress Catalog Card Number: 80-81685

ACKNOWLEDGMENTS

This book took us over three years to write. During that time, we received no encouragement from Foundations and Survivors' Organizations.

However, certain people were at our side at all times, and their kind words and sincere interest inspired us to continue and complete this book. We must first mention Samuel and Arleen Rudski. Words are insufficient to express our gratitude to this sincere couple who were always ready with a word of encouragement. They really believed in our project and their faith kept our morale up during many dark days.

The late Samuel Rajzman, one of the leaders of the Treblinka uprising, encouraged us with what was almost his last breath. He believed that our work was a legacy for future generations, and we regret that he died before he could see the book in print.

Hilda Roiter sacrificed her family Sundays for over three years and was forced to listen for interminable hours to animated Yiddish conversations which she didn't understand. We thank her for her patience and understanding.

We thank Mr. Isaac Piasetski, Chairman of the Eastern Region Holocaust Education Committee of the Canadian Jewish Congress, for his interest. He brought both of us together. Professor Yakov Rabkin of the Université de Montréal offered his editorial skill and valuable time, and we appreciate his contribution.

N. Kohn
H. Roiter

PREFACE

The story of the Jewish partisans during World War II is a largely neglected chapter of Holocaust history. The story of organized Jewish resistance to Nazi terror has crystallized around the Warsaw ghetto uprising, the Bialystok uprising, the Vilna area resistance, the Treblinka, Sobibor, and Auschwitz revolts, and a few other incidents. This emphasis, however, provides a very fragmentary picture of the actual scale and heroism of Jewish resistance.

There are a number of reasons for the neglect of Jewish partisan activity. Postwar political considerations are one cause of this neglect. The Nazis were the supreme rulers of an area stretching from Narvik in Norway to the African Sahara. Only the protection provided by the English Channel allowed the British to carry on the fight from their isolated island. The Jews, of course, were the primary target of the Nazis, and the Eastern European Jews remained under the Nazi heel for a relatively long period. The naive, optimistic Jew, used to anti-Semitism and discrimination, was systematically duped until he was a near-skeleton. He was stripped of his leadership and intelligentsia, and then his family was taken from him too. However, many of those skeletons gathered in cellars, bunkers, and forests and fought the Nazi giants. Theirs was a hopeless fight, and they knew it, but they pursued their goal of revenge with determination and courage. They were surrounded by largely hostile populations, so they lacked supply sources, and they were generally of urban or semi-urban origin, so the forest was alien to them. And yet they fought, against enormous and prohibitive odds, and the vast majority of them were annihilated. The following pages mention, in passing, the existence of a 50-man Jewish fighting group in the Volhynia area led by an Ignatovka schoolteacher. This group was lured into a trap and betrayed by Polish villagers, and every single member of it perished. They accomplished things, those bedraggled Moishes and Yankels with their schoolteacher leader. Kohn heard about their deeds, as did other resistance leaders in the area. And yet, if not for Nahum Kohn's testimony, their very existence as a fighting group would remain unknown.

What we know of Jewish partisan groups in Eastern Europe comes from those partisans who reached the West after the war. Thus we know of the mighty deeds of Abba Kovner, Dr. Jehezkiel Atlas, Hirsh Kaplinski, the Bielski brothers, Misha Gildenman ("Dyadya Misha"), Yitzhak Rudnicki and many others. However, this is but a fraction of the true story of the Jewish resistance, and the rest must be rescued from oblivion while survivors and eyewitnesses still live. After their departure, it will be too late.

Nahum Kohn, a small-town Jewish watchmaker from a religious family has worked at his trade since the age of 13. In 1939, his native town Sieradz, in Western Poland, had 5,000 Jews, about 40% of the total population. It was occupied by the Germans on the third day of the war (Sept. 3, 1939), a ghetto was established on March 1, 1940, and by the beginning of 1942 only 1200 of them remained, to be exterminated in August 1942 in Chelmno death camp.

Kohn found himself, at the beginning of the Russo-German war, far from his native Sieradz. He was in the Volhynia area of the Ukraine, a displaced person even before hostilities started. Kohn, an essentially straightforward and pragmatic man, quickly perceived that the Nazis and their Ukrainian henchmen were intent on exterminating the Jews. He also understood that the forest offered the only chance of organizing some armed resistance, so, with his one-half day of military training, he took to the woods and organized an eighteen-man group of fighting Jewish youth. This group, which actively and heroically engaged the enemy for nearly a year, was almost completely wiped out by the Germans. Kohn himself learned only in 1945 about the final moments of his boys; by coincidence, he ran into a survivor of his group who had been severely wounded, and this survivor told him what had happened.

Kohn, after three months of searching, found the antifascist resistance group led by a noble Ukrainian, Aleksandr Fyodorovich Felyuk, and he became a member of this group. On a canvas that is dark and bloody, Aleksandr Fyodorovich Felyuk shines forth like a beacon. This sensitive and idealistic Gentile incorporated in himself the finest and highest human traits, when the whole world around him had become drunk with Jewish blood. If the following pages manage to do only one thing, to preserve the deeds and behavior of a Felyuk for future generations, then this book will have served a valuable purpose.

After being severely wounded, Kohn joined the official Soviet partisan *atrád* (unit; *lit.*, "detachment") led by D. M. Medvedev. This atrád, the most famous Soviet partisan atrád in World War II, specialized in intelligence activities, and Kohn became one of those who were privileged to help the famous infiltrator Kuznetsov in his vital activities. No German general in the Rovno area could sleep safely while Medvedev's men were in the vicinity, and many senior German generals met their justly merited ends at the hands of

[9]

Kuznetsov and his associates. Extremely important military intelligence was ferreted out by Medvedev's atrád and transmitted to Moscow. Kohn's alias was Mietek (Misha) Kowalski.

From the end of the war until 1955, little was said or written in the Soviet Union about the great accomplishment of the partisans. The Red Army was given virtually all the credit for the victory over the Nazis. However, in 1955, when the role of the Red Army in the victory was justifiably secure, attention was focused on the partisan movement. Books appeared, movies were made, and plays were performed about the partisans. Nahum Kohn was decorated by the Soviet authorities on many occasions, and he was invited to speak about Medvedev's partisans on an almost weekly basis to school, youth, and veterans' groups.

He married a Jewish woman in 1950 and they have 2 daughters, Helena and Olga. Helena recently received her Master's in music from McGill, and is an accomplished pianist. Olga, who is also very talented, is still studying music. Mr. Kohn applied 5 times to leave the Soviet Union (the first application was made in 1948–9) and he was refused each time. When Kosygin visited Ottawa in the early 1970's Canadian Prime Minister Trudeau handed him a list of Canadian families who wanted to be reunited with their Soviet relatives. Kohn's brother Felix had managed to get Kohn placed on that list, and one week after Kosygin's return to the Soviet Union Kohn was told that he would be allowed to emigrate together with his wife and two children. He came to Canada in 1972.

One thing, however, bothered Kohn. The official Soviet archives cover his activities from the moment he joined Felyuk's group until the end of the war, but, the Soviet authorities refused to include his eighteen-man Jewish group in the record. Kohn made repeated requests, and he was rebuffed each time although the authorities were fully aware of the courageous deeds of Kohn's boys. The following pages thus constitute a form of monument to Avram Druker, Chaim Klein, Kalman Klein, Yitzhak der Melchiger, Schwartz, Shuster, Avraimele, and the others, who have no known graves and no monument. They are mentioned in no books, and they have nobody to recite the memorial prayers for them. They fought, however, for the dignity of their people and the cause of human dignity, and they deserve a better fate than oblivion.

The following pages, told firsthand by the man who lived them, are designed to give the reader a *total* picture of one Jewish partisan's life. How does an essentially urban man go into the woods and survive? How does he manage to obtain arms and carry the fight to the enemy? What did he eat? Where did he sleep?

I firmly believe that his story should be known, especially by young people. Every word in the manuscript is *true*. Kohn is a simple man, not an intellectual, of the very highest personal integrity. For a Jew to have been honored like he was in the Soviet Union (where he was not a Communist Party member) speaks for itself.

We can do nothing to alter the past. However, we can try to preserve it and, by preserving it, share in a small way in the story of our past which is, after all, at the root of our present.

Howard Roiter

PART ONE

I will tell you about a world that went crazy, a world where humans became beasts, life turned worthless, and the forest became "home." And I also will tell you about people who refused to surrender to bestiality, people who resisted the descent into darkness. Most of them are gone, but I see them still, in their tattered rags, city boys darting from tree to tree in the forest, repaying death with death. I, too, was a city boy, and although I survived, I have never really left those forests. They will be with me till my last breath.

When the war broke out in September 1939, I was in Warsaw. I was given an old rifle, hurriedly taught how to use it, and stationed at a Mokotowska Street barricade. When Warsaw fell, I returned to my sister Helena's apartment at 32 Twarda Street, and then I made my way back to my home town, Sieradz, near the Polish-German border. I was one of twelve brothers and sisters, and my father, a religious Jew, supported the family with his hardware store.

When I came home, they told me that six or seven Jews had been killed and that it was dangerous to go out between certain hours, but no ghetto had been established yet. At that time I was the oldest son in the house (although the girls were all older), since my older brother was in the Polish Army and we hadn't heard from him for a while. In Sieradz, Jewish boys of my age had already been seized for forced labor. After I was a month at home and had fully recovered from some injuries I had received during the saturation bombing of Warsaw, the Germans published an order: the Jews had to put on Star of David patches, and if a Jew were found without a patch they would shoot him on sight. The following day, Sunday, we were all busy putting on those patches.

That very same Sunday, my friend Mulish Jakubovich, who was my age or perhaps a year older, came into our yard. (Polish homes were built around an inner yard.) He said, "You know, they say the Russian Army has approached the Bug River, and many people are crossing over to the Russian side. Let's go and cross over ourselves." I had to tell him that since I was now the oldest son at home, I had certain responsibilities and would have to consult my parents and the other members of my family. So he said, "All right. I'll speak to you in an hour."

The members of my family were all sitting around the table; every child had his or her own place, and my father sat at the head of the table in the traditional way. I spoke respectfully to my father and told him that Mulish had proposed that we cross the Bug River into Russian-held territory. My father wouldn't commit himself. He said, "You're almost twenty-one years old. You have to make up your own mind." But my mother was firm. She immediately said, "You must go! A young person like you must get out of here!" And my sister Sara said the same thing, "You shouldn't remain here one minute more!" As we were discussing this matter, Mulish came in with his valise. I told him, "I can't decide because I haven't my father's approval." Then my father spoke up. "Go! You're young. Get as far away as possible!" I thought: Where should we go? We must return 200 kilometers to Warsaw and from there cross the bridge to Praga. There we would have to find some way of getting to the Bug. By this time Jews were not permitted to ride on the trains.

My youngest sister was a seamstress, and she had made the Star of David patches for all of us. Mine was sewn on my clothes already. We were discussing this at around 9 P.M., and the train was to leave at 11 P.M. When I determined to go, I decided I wouldn't wear the patch, and I ripped it off. I would take the carriage to the train station without wearing the patch. And that's the way I proceeded.

My father had come from Warsaw, his parents were natives of Warsaw, and he had sisters there. He said, "Take two valises and go to your Aunt Chava in Warsaw." Mother had already packed my things. At the station, we couldn't buy tickets because we were Jews, so we paid a Pole to get us two tickets to Warsaw. We left Sieradz on the very day the Jews had to put on their Star of David patches.

On the train, various unpleasant incidents took place. They were looking for Jews, and when they spotted a Jew they threw him off the speeding train. At that time they were going by faces, and since my face didn't look very Jewish, I escaped these spot checks avidly carried out by Germans and Poles. Yes, the Poles were certainly helping! Had it not been for the "helpers" there couldn't have been a Holocaust. That's my own opinion, but it's one I hold quite firmly.

When we arrived in Warsaw, we spent the night with my aunt. The next morning we crossed the bridge to Praga and bought tickets for Malkinia, a town near the border. As the train approached Malkinia, the Germans stopped the train, surrounded it, chased everybody off, and divided them into three separate groups: Ukrainians, Poles, and Jews. The Germans used dogs. They were yelling and shouting, and here I was separated from my friend Mulish. It was night, hundreds of people were milling about, and I couldn't see him anywhere. I looked for him for several hours. I couldn't decide whether to join the Polish or Jewish group, but I

[17]

figured that Mulish must have been with the Jews, so I went over to the Jewish group. Many Jews had slipped into the Polish group. The Jews were standing in three rows "supervised" by three Germans, who were searching and beating. One of the Germans looked half-decent, so I moved into his row. Just before I left home my sister had sewn some money into my shoulder pads. I was sure that the German would find this money, so I ripped out the shoulder pads and threw them away. I figured that if it wouldn't be mine then it wouldn't be theirs either. I had a knapsack with a change of clothes, a hat, an extra pair of shoes, and a couple of shirts; I also had a small valise with my watchmaker's tools. The German came over and asked me what I had. I showed him the shirts, some bread, the shoes. I explained to him that the tools in the small valise were my watchmaker's tools. He asked, "You have money?" I said, "Yes. I have ten zlotys in one pocket and a hundred and fifty in the other." He asked, "Don't you have any more?" I replied negatively. He put his hand into my jacket and took out a letter that I hadn't even known about. I explained that this must be the address of my father's friend, an address I could turn to. So the German let me go. I went off to the side a bit, and two Germans came over and gave me several good blows. I bore up well, because I was in very good shape. I had always been very active in sports, and that helped me a great deal in my life. After these blows, I walked down to the border area.

This border area, 200 meters in width, was a neutral zone. It was neither German nor Russian. I remained there several days. I called out loud for my friend Mulish, but I couldn't find him. People there said that the Russians used to let people cross over easily, but now it had become more difficult. You had to sneak across now. I went into a little wooded area full of groups of people huddling together —

family groups, groups of friends, people from the same towns, and so on. When I woke up one morning, I noticed that a group that had been sitting in a certain place was gone. And other groups who were there the previous evening had also disappeared. I knew they must have crossed over to the Russian side. I was all alone, however. After several nights I decided that I would not fall asleep. I'd lie down near a certain group. During the night I saw them get up quietly and move off. I thought to follow them, but in the woods I lost them. When I lost them, I lost my bearings completely.

It was the first time I had been in a forest, and this was night, too. Fearing that I would return to the Germans, I oriented myself as best I could, and moved in what I hoped was the general direction of the Russians. As dawn was breaking, two men suddenly accosted me. I don't know whether they were Polish or Ukrainian; they spoke half-Polish, half-Ukrainian, and I had never heard Ukrainian before. They tried to rip the valise out of my hand. I was young and healthy, so when one of them hit me I hit him back. One of them took out a knife and tried to stab me, so I grabbed his hand. He lost his grip on the valise handle but then tried to stab me in the face. As I deflected his thrust, the blade went into my shoulder. I succeeded in escaping from them, but I had walked scarcely 100 meters when I suddenly became very dizzy. An artery had been severed, and I had to cut off a piece of my shirt and tie the wound up. Another 100 meters brought me to a road with movement on it. There I raised my hand, and a Russian military vehicle stopped. Seeing my wound, they took me on board. I had never heard Russian before, but one of the soldiers was Jewish and started speaking Yiddish to me. They took me to a small hamlet called Czyzew, where I was put in the local infirmary. I remained there for a little over a week.

From Czyzew I went to Bialystok, only to find thousands of refugees milling around. Where would I sleep the first night? It was cold then — more than two months had passed since the war started. I went to a synagogue. My father wasn't a fanatic, but he was a religious man. I had gone to a *cheder* (traditional religious primary school) until I was 10 years old, so I felt somewhat at home in a religious milieu. There were thousands of people in that synagogue. There was no room at all to sit down there, and stretching out seemed out of the question. However, I remained there for several days and went to watchmakers to look for work. Some didn't want to employ refugees from Poland; others wanted a character reference, and I didn't know a soul there.

After two days, I ran out of money, so I sold my hat. I went out to the local market and held out my hat; somebody came over and made me an offer. He gave me his old hat in return and some money. I went into a restaurant, and as I entered I heard "Nahum! Nahum!" There were two friends from my hometown, Yukish and Chanchi Valdman (they're now in Israel). We were very happy to see each other, and they told me that there were more people from Sieradz in Bialystok. They mentioned several names, including my cousin Nachi Gliksman. And then they told me the best news: "Somebody saw your brother Laizer in Kovel, only about a hundred fifty kilometers from Bialystok." So I set off for Kovel, where I looked in vain for Laizer for several days. But again I met a *landsman* (somebody from one's home town) named Schnurek, who said that he had heard that my brother was in Lutsk. What should I do? I was tired; I hadn't changed my clothes for several weeks. It was the first time I had been away from home like that, on the road, and I wasn't used to that kind of abnormal existence. But if one had seen him in Kovel, another in Lutsk, Laizer must be in the area. And I wanted desperately to be with my own kin — after all, a brother is a brother. So I took the train to Lutsk.

Coming off the train at five in the morning, I didn't know where to go. I didn't know Lutsk at all, and I was exhausted. Seeing a watch repair shop near the train station, I thought I would wait until the watchmaker came to open his shop. I sat down on the threshold and fell asleep.

Later somebody gently woke me. A man said, "What are you doing here?" I said nothing; I was still half asleep, disoriented. He said, "What are you sleeping here for?" I replied, "I'm a watchmaker. I'm looking for work." He looked me over carefully, and I felt a certain fraternal warmth in his look. This watchmaker, Shloime Mechlin, was a short fellow, about 45–50 years old. He opened the door, led me into the back of his shop where he lived, took a look at me, and said, "First come in and wash yourself, and then we'll talk." I was ashamed. It was the first time I was out of the house, like an ordinary drifter, and I couldn't accept his offer of food. So he said, "Take a nap, and then come out to the front, to my shop." This I agreed to. When I washed and fell asleep, I slept a whole day.

When I woke up the next day, I felt reassured because I saw the Sabbath candlesticks. I saw that this was a house where religion was respected. He offered me food, and I hesitated again. With great compassion and understanding, Mechlin said to me, "Look, if you don't want to eat here, don't — but here's some money. Go buy yourself something to eat. You're going to die from starvation if you continue to fast!" When I returned, he asked me, "What kind of watch repairing ability do you have? Can you repair a large alarm clock?" I said, "Yes." He tested me. He gave me one, and I repaired it. "Can you fix a pocket watch?" I fixed one for him too. The next day he asked me, "How much salary do you

want?" I said, "I just want a place to sleep and some food."
He looked at me and shook his head. "Listen to me, Kohn.
You're in trouble now. That's why you just want food and
shelter. I don't want to take advantage of you. I'm going to
give you food, shelter, and eight rubles a day." So that was
the agreement we made, and I worked for Shloime Mechlin
for two weeks.

After two weeks, I told Mr. Mechlin that I didn't want to
work that day, that I wanted to find my brother. He tried his
utmost to dissuade me; he begged me not to go. But when he
saw that there was no budging me, he said, "Listen, I took
you in because in World War I, I was a displaced person, a
refugee, in Austria. I wandered around for many months
before I found work. You reminded me of my past. So
please, don't get lost. Come back. You have a place with us."
Yes, Shloime Mechlin was a very fine man. And he really felt
for me.

I went out on the street — Jagiellonska — a very long
street. It was later renamed Stalin Street. After walking quite
a distance, I turned right and came to a very big bridge called
the Krasne Bridge. I stationed myself at one end of the
bridge to look at the people crossing. Incredibly, I saw somebody who, from the back, seemed to walk like my brother
Laizer. He was wearing a Polish military overcoat. I began to
follow him amid the cars and the crowds, afraid of losing him
but hesitant to call his name. Could it really be Laizer? As I
approached, I saw his face, and I shouted, "Laizer! Laizer!"
He turned around. Well — you can imagine the crying; how
we hugged each other. I told him all the latest news from
home. He told me that our uncle from Lodz, Shtulman, was
living in Lutsk, along with our cousins Morris and Ruzha
Vrotzlavsky. They were all living together and Laizer had
joined them.

[22]

I went with my brother and stayed with them for two weeks, but the way I had abandoned Mr. Mechlin and his family began to bother me. My uncle felt that I owed it to the watchmaker to return to him, so I went back. They were all crying when they saw me. They thought I had disappeared, but I told them how I had found my brother. I worked for Mr. Mechlin until it was prohibited for him to keep employees. You see, under the Russians he was allowed to work on his own, but he wasn't allowed to have paid help. I worked with Mechlin for three or four months, into the beginning of 1940, and from there I went to work at a state-run watchmakers' collective. One evening, however, the refugees were all gathered together and shipped off to Siberia. We were put aboard a train, but before it had moved very far, a number of us jumped off and hid in a forest for five or six days.

We returned to Lutsk because we already knew people there and spent a week or two hiding in a livery stable. Among the refugees were a watchmaker, Kalman Klein, from my home town, and his older brother. We all remained together, but we saw that we would have to find work. I went to the local militia and explained that I was seeking work. They asked who I was, where I was from. When I replied, the official looked at my papers and understood that I wasn't supposed to be there. When he asked how I came to be there, I gave him a cock-and-bull story. He replied, "All right. But you're not allowed to work in Lutsk. About 30 kilometers from here there's a small town, Tsuman. You may work there." I returned to my friends and told them what the official had advised.

Back at the livery stable, the stable owner had another idea. "What do you need to go to Tsuman for? Near Tsuman, there are two villages of Jewish peasants. Once a week my friend, the community leader there, visits me. I'll mention you to him, and we'll try to arrange something." He did come, this community leader. His name was Shuster, and he discussed things with me. These two Jewish villages were located deep in the forest. One village, Trochenbrot, had 500 families and the other village, Ignatovka, had 120 families. When we arrived there, it was the first time in my life that I saw Jewish farmers. I could never have imagined this, and I rejoiced when I saw them. Most of them worked the fields; some of them worked leather. Everybody had primitive leather-working equipment at home, and they worked on the hides. So they lived from their fields, their cows, their horses, and their hides. They were totally surrounded by forests; the nearest road was twenty or thirty kilometers away. I was curious, so I used to ask old-timers how they came to be there. They told me that the area had been totally unsettled and wild; their ancestors had been exiled there by the first tsars as a punishment for refusing military service.

We remained there for several months. With our watch repairing skills, my friend Kalman Klein and I could earn something. The people in Trochenbrot-Ignatovka didn't have wristwatches, but they had ancient clocks on their walls, and before our arrival there had been no watchmaker. So they brought these antiques to us and bartered food in exchange for repairs. I was there with my brother Laizer, Kalman Klein was with his brother, and then another refugee joined us. We lived collectively; whatever we earned went, literally, into the common pot.

After a month or two, my cousin Simcha and his brother joined us. My father, in a letter I had received when I was still in Warsaw, had asked me to look after Simcha like my own brother. Even when I was in Lutsk with my brother, and later in Trochenbrot-Ignatovka, we had postal contact with our parents. My father was in the Warsaw ghetto, and my mother was in Sieradz. We sent packages, most of them to Warsaw. In Sieradz, because it was a smaller town, my family could get by, more or less. But in Warsaw there was greater need. Every month we sent a package. The packages caused hardships for us because they were very expensive. A kilogram of butter cost twenty rubles. I could send eight kilos altogether. Sending chocolates was allowed. I also sent animal fat, since in Warsaw it could be exchanged for many potatoes. We sent these packages until the war broke out in June of 1941.

Why was my father in Warsaw? In Sieradz, when things became bad, men from 20 to 55 years old were seized for forced labor. My father was a native of Warsaw and had his sisters there as well. The family decided that life would be easier in Warsaw, so they went there voluntarily. They had to smuggle their way across 200 kilometers, because Jews were not permitted to travel. But several months after they arrived, the ghetto was established, and everybody was locked in. With great difficulty, my mother and the children got out; but they couldn't get my father out. Some time later, he was brought back to Sieradz by a local German named Berger.

My father was helped greatly by Berger, a German who was born in Sieradz. Berger was a mechanic; he had his shop on the Rogatka (the street leading to the railroad station.) Even as a child I remember how friendly Berger was with my father. They used to discuss political and personal problems; they used to confide in each other. When the war came, Berger really demonstrated what a *mentsch* (a real human being) he was. When the war started, he helped my father in Warsaw. When he saw that further help was no longer possible, he made a plan to get my father out of the Warsaw ghetto and bring him back to Sieradz. Berger, accompanied by my sister Sara, went near Warsaw, and he alone "talked things over" with the Germans and Jewish police. He succeeded in bringing my father back to Sieradz. However, I was told that five or six months later the Germans found out about this, and they took this Berger out and shot him. He deserves to be remembered, this elderly Berger — a man with a concept of friendship and decency that led him to pay the supreme price for his humanity.

Before the war, Berger used to eat very often at our house. He used especially to love Jewish-style fish. He often used to turn up on Fridays for the Sabbath fish. My mother would serve him a portion or two of fish, a glass of whiskey, and some challah (Sabbath bread). Berger used to sit for an hour or an hour and a half; he would eat, chat, gossip a bit, and then he would leave. This ritual went on as far back as I can remember.

Once, in the 1930's, when he came by, my mother was busy with something, so she said, "Go to the kitchen; you know where everything is — make yourself a snack." My mother used to use more Polish in talking with Berger; my father used more German. So Berger went to the kitchen, where his snack was to have taken him half an hour, or an hour. When almost two hours passed, and he was not back, my mother went into the kitchen. She saw that he was lying unconscious on the floor. Foam was bubbling from his lips. My mother was very frightened; Berger looked dead. She called the doctor, who arrived quickly. Meanwhile, a crowd had gathered, and the word got around that the Jews had poisoned a German. They started to beat Jews on the streets. Berger was taken to the hospital, where they probably pumped out his stomach. It took half a day till he came to himself. He explained what had happened: he had come alone into the kitchen, and in the pantry there were two bottles of clear liquid, one of whiskey (spiritus) and another of vinegar. He took the vinegar instead of the spiritus. When he explained this, the mob quieted down. However, until he spoke up, Jews had to stay off the streets.

I also had contact with Sieradz. I corresponded with my sister Sara. The boys in the family used to call her momma, for she was a second mother to us. If I wanted to eat, I didn't go to my mother — I went to Sara. When I returned from school, Sara used to check my homework, my marks. I would get both slaps and kisses from her. A week or two before the war broke out I received the last letter from Sara. Half the letter had been blacked out by the censor, but from the remainder I extracted the following message: "Go far, far away from us, as far as possible; don't stay still because we are going to see you soon. And we don't want to see you at all." I couldn't understand it at first, but later it dawned on me. She saw that the German military machine was going into high gear; there were movements towards the border. That was my last letter from home.

Our collective life in Trochenbrot-Ignatovka lasted until four or five months before the Russian-German war broke out. My cousin Simcha said that we should retreat deep into Russia, but my brother didn't want to go, and I wouldn't go without him. Simcha left, so Laizer and I and Kalman Klein and his brother were left. We went finally to Tsuman, where we opened a watch-repair shop. My brother started to work in a lumber mill.

One night we heard heavy shooting. We had no radios, but when we woke up in the morning, it seemed the Christians already knew. News of war spreads fast, although at the lumber mill they still said it was a false alarm. The first word that came through was that the Russians had penetrated deep into German territory. I figured it was impossible. The next day we decided to retreat with the Russians. Although we covered 150 kilometers, the Germans had outstripped us, and we were once again under the German heel. We returned to Tsuman, but we couldn't stay there longer than two days, for the Germans immediately stated that any Jews found in Tsuman would be shot on sight. Had we remained there, we would have been highly visible. Before the war there were no Jews at all living there. Now there were Kalman Klein and his brother, Laizer and I, and five or six other refugees. So back we went to the Jewish villages of Trochenbrot-Ignatovka.

I had very few illusions. My sister Sara's letters were clear enough. She used a simple code. "That one went away" meant that he had been killed. Her letters stated repeatedly that "this one went away . . . that one went away . . . another one went away." They had all been killed. When I was still at home, the Germans had already taken "volunteers" to the Lublin area for "labor duty." Near Lublin they established one of the first concentration camps. I didn't know it meant extermination, but there were rumors. And now, in Trochenbrot-Ignatovka, we were surrounded by Ukrainian villages; 90 percent of the inhabitants were Ukrainian nationalists. They used to come into Trochenbrot to pillage, rob, loot, and rape. The Jews had no protection. A dog had more rights than a Jew. It didn't occur to me yet that the Germans had planned complete extermination, but I saw that they and their Ukrainian nationalist collaborators had complete freedom to do whatever they pleased. I said, "Why should we let such scum do whatever they want? Let's do something on our own; let's at least preserve some freedom of action!" My friend Kalman Klein supported me strongly, so we decided to go into the woods to see what life was possible there. We would still have continual contact with Trochenbrot, but in the forest we could organize, and then perhaps we would be able to do something, carry on some resistance. I knew nothing about military matters, but I saw that there was only one course of action possible: fighting. And Trochenbrot-Ignatovka *was* surrounded completely by dark forests.

I suggested to Kalman that we should take young people into the forest and form big groups — the bigger the better. We would rescue as many young people as we could and take revenge for the innocent Jewish blood that had been shed. Many people laughed at this idea, but I knew the young people of Trochenbrot. I had faith in them. It was a golden youth, idealistic and unsophisticated; they were peasants. I must admit that the local Jewish population was *strongly* against us. They said, "First of all, the Germans are not killing. And what would the Germans want with us? Our grandfathers were working this land. We have no bad relations with anybody; we are farmers." But they forgot that just the word Jew was enough — it meant extermination. This they couldn't understand. Many times we would quietly gather the young people. But the community leaders found out and came after us with sticks, remonstrating, "Because of you we will suffer. You have nothing to lose — you're homeless, you're refugees, you're displaced persons — but we have our houses, our fields, our property. We have a lot to lose!" So I didn't accomplish very much with these clandestine gatherings.

My brother agreed that we would have to get arms. He said we should prepare arms caches in Trochenbrot, while I argued that the caches should be located in the forest, because only there could we properly organize ourselves. Frankly, we didn't know what to expect. We thought a few policemen would come, two or three Germans, and they would kill a few Jews. None of us could even imagine the magnitude of what would come later. My brother wanted to remain in Trochenbrot; only Kalman supported me fully. Two or three days after the community leaders broke up our recruiting efforts, Kalman and I went permanently into the forest. First one fellow joined us; then a second came, and then a third. I had contact with my brother, who still wanted me to rejoin him in Trochenbrot. I wanted him to join us. I was stubborn, however. Laizer had been in the army; he knew how to fight, and we knew nothing — we were rank amateurs. My Warsaw training had taken minutes, not hours. My brother had served his full term in the Polish army and had been on major maneuvers.

We were overjoyed when he finally decided to join us in the forest. For me it was a double joy; my brother would be at my side. We told him he would instruct us in the proper use of arms, tactics, and the rest, all to be practiced in a proper military way. Unfortunately, Laizer was with us only eight or nine days. He was wounded in our first fight with the Ukrainian nationalist police. He was wounded in the hand; it wasn't a bad wound, but it was a wound. And we had no medical supplies in the woods, only some animal fats and primitive bandages. So we decided that, to avoid infection, Laizer would return to Trochenbrot for one week, where a *feldsher* (medic) — more like half a *feldsher* — would take care of my brother. So Laizer was brought back to town, his hand was rebandaged, and he seemed to be getting along well. However, before the week was out, the Judenrat (Jewish community council) officials came at night and took a quota of men for "work." Ignatovka had to supply 20 men, and Trochenbrot 150 men. Laizer was one of those taken.

In the forest, many boys appeared from scattered Jewish villages. They said that many Judenrat members were not honest men — an honest Jew couldn't remain long on such a

which was producing little packets of butter for the German military forces at the front. It was guarded by several police. We made a wreck of the place, and then burned it down. We lost two people there, but we killed a number of Germans and Ukrainian nationalist police, and we took three persons with us. We couldn't keep prisoners, but we needed information, and they were a prime source. We didn't keep them more than two or three hours. After the questioning, they paid for the innocent Jewish blood they had shed.

This was our work and our life. The Germans knew about us, but they couldn't catch us. Today we were here, tomorrow we were far away, and on the third day we were even further than that. In our general area there were, besides my group, many Jewish groups in the forest — one of ten men, another of twenty men, and so on — but most were killed to the last man. They met their end because they weren't well organized, lacked good operational tactics, and had too much trust in other humans. The peasants would lure them into traps. I heard of a Jewish group of fifty men who were all slaughtered because of a Polish village, Pshebrazhe. They had close contact with Pshebrazhe, and they had confidence in the townspeople. One day, these townspeople invited them in, tipped off the authorities, and that was the end of that group. I could never make contact with that specific group. In fact, we had no real contact with any of those other Jewish groups operating in the vicinity.

The Germans were very strong at that time; they were confident. They were the masters — the world was theirs. There were no Russian partisans — nobody had heard of any such thing. But I had heard of a group of Gentiles who were battling the Germans and the Ukrainian nationalists in our vicinity. I searched for this group too, without success, for many months.

We never remained long in one place — one day, or two at

the very most. We moved according to our instincts. You develop that kind of instinct in the woods. Sleeping comfort was not too important, since we rarely slept in the same place twice. We would dig individual holes half a meter deep, line them with moss, post a rotating guard, and sleep. If we were ten people, only half of us could sleep at the same time. There were two men on an inner watch detail, and two or three men on an outer watch detail. Time taught us how to survive in the woods, but more than that, the forest really became my home. When I returned to the woods after a mission, I felt as if I were coming home. I felt completely at home in "my" forests.

Sometimes we would make a very small fire and warm ourselves around it. The worst thing was that we couldn't change our clothes, which meant we were covered with lice. But we found an answer to that problem. We would hold our clothes over a fire, far enough away that the clothes didn't burn, but close enough to roast the lice.

We would move into the hostile villages at night. We would go into a peasant's hut to seize a collaborator, and he would tell us things. Part was true and part was lies. After a while we learned to separate the truth from the lies.

At the beginning, when we passed a village or hamlet, it was my policy that we try to avoid being noticed. My group was small, and if we were on our way to a mission, I didn't want any strangers to see our movements. Also, we were still quite green, with little actual combat experience. When the Ukrainian nationalists saw a Jew, they automatically assumed he was completely helpless and passive — an easy target. So when they saw us, they used to pursue us with sticks, knives, and, more often, axes. I tried to avoid an open battle with them because we had more important quarrels to settle.

But this harassment went on for weeks, and I saw that it was getting worse. Discussing it with Kalman, I said, "This can't be allowed to continue! We have to do something about this harassment, or we'll end up as do-nothings confined to the forest." I continued, "We'll go through the main streets, at noon, of every village that lies on our path to a mission, and the villagers who attack us will get theirs. We'll pay them back with a dose of their own medicine. We'll teach them a little about respect for their fellow humans."

And that's the way it was. A few days later, we sent four men through the center of a hamlet, Silno. A dozen more of us hid a short distance away. When the Silno inhabitants perceived our four men, they jumped out and started shrieking with joy, "Jews, Jews — what fun! Let's get at them, boys!" And they started shooting. The rest of us then moved into the village and returned the fire. They were taken aback by our real numbers and our resistance, so they took shelter in a hut. A thirty-minute firefight followed. Bullets were flying hot and thick, and one of our bullets set the hut on fire. We watched it burn, and we made sure that nobody escaped from the flames. We made our case well that day — the great-grandchildren of these Silno inhabitants wouldn't forget our message.

Several other incidents took place then. In one case, when we found out that a certain peasant led the attacks on us, we swooped down on his house, sent the women and children out, sat him down, and asked him point blank, "Why do you behave like that? What secret thrill do you get when you pursue ragged Jews?" We pieced together what he had done to innocent Jewish refugees who had wandered into his town. I couldn't control my boys; one jumped on him with a stick, and another beat him with a piece of iron. I finally managed to stop them. I said, "He wanted to kill us, so let's kill him and be done with it!" So we took him out to the back of the house and shot him.

After these incidents, our problem disappeared. We could

[37]

go through any village or hamlet, by day or night — even in broad daylight. When the villagers saw us coming, they would close their windows, fasten their shutters, lock their doors, and sit as still as mice, praying that we would leave them in peace. This taught us a valuable lesson: with certain kinds of human beings, you mustn't be passive. You have to be a "giver" too — that's the only language they understand.

We couldn't do our work without precise information, and much of it was obtained from friends of our members. When we came into a village, we couldn't search for the Jew-killers — we had to know exactly where they were. Still, we weren't afraid to stay most of the night in a village. We would post a guard on the outskirts of the village, and while two or three men went in, the rest took up planned key positions. We had previously decided where we'd come in and where we'd go out of the village. Experience taught us. Had we learned from books alone, we probably would have been finished off sooner. Practice and theory are two entirely different things. At the beginning, because we lacked practical experience we lost several men we shouldn't have lost.

Avram Druker joined us after the first massacre of Jews in Trochenbrot-Ignatovka. He had lived in Ignatovka, a kilometer or half a kilometer from Trochenbrot. That first massacre took place in 1942, at the beginning of summer. The Germans and their Ukrainian nationalist helpers surrounded the place, assembled their victims, and machine-gunned them to death. A few days later we ran into Avram Druker in the woods; he was a wide-shouldered 16-year-old. He said he had been looking for us before the massacre but couldn't find us. He was overjoyed to see us. We took him into our group, although he didn't have any arms with him and we had none to give him.

Druker told us about a Ukrainian nationalist policeman,

[38]

Ponas, who lived in Domasov, a village near Trochenbrot. Druker described how Ponas helped the Germans kill Jews. Ponas had taken Druker's sister and her child out of their house and shot them in the yard. So Druker asked for permission to go to Domasov, settle up for his sister's and nephew's lives, and take Ponas' rifle. We wouldn't let him go alone. We made an exact plan, considering carefully the number of policemen stationed there, their positions and so forth. We gave Avram a revolver and taught him how to use it. Four men went with him, with Kalman Klein as their leader. When they approached the house, Druker saw Ponas sitting at a table. Kalman Klein whispered that they would go in and take this murderer out alive, but Druker was too eager. The window was very low, so he jumped through it, flung himself on Ponas' throat, and bit through his jugular. Our other men then went in and took Ponas' rifle. So that's how Avram Druker settled up for his sister and her child. Ponas' career as a Jew-killer came to an abrupt and well-merited end.

When Avram returned with the other men, they described to me what had happened. I went to him and said, "Listen, Avram. Here everybody must follow orders. If you do such a thing again . . . ." He suddenly started to cry terribly. I asked him why he was crying. "I wanted to kill Ponas' wife too, but Kalman Klein wouldn't let me." I explained, "Ponas was guilty, but his wife may have been innocent." I had to make him understand. "Avram, you must follow orders, or you may be the downfall of all of us." He obviously took my warning to heart, because he was with us for eight months, and in every battle he excelled like a veteran.

Avram brought us another piece of information. There was a wooden grain mill near Ignatovka, operated by a man of German origin, named Yuleks. In World War I, when the

Russians chased the Germans back, Yuleks had remained behind and married a Polish girl from the area. In the 1920's, the Jews from this area, who grew corn and wheat, had had to travel thirty kilometers to the nearest mill to grind their grain. So nine Jewish partners got together to build a mill. One of the partners was Druker's father. Druker explained that Yuleks didn't kill Jews personally, but blackmailed them. Since he knew exactly what they had, he bled them white. He took gold, diamonds — whatever he could get. When these poor, terrified and terrorized Jews had nothing left to give, he handed them over to the Germans, who shot them. Druker described how his own aunt had been blackmailed by Yuleks, and he described many other similar incidents. He kept his own hands ostensibly clean; he stood at a distance and let the Germans do his dirty work.

We decided that Yuleks must be taken alive. We had to put him on trial; he had to know why he was being killed. There were cases where we killed immediately, but where it was at all possible we tried — even if we had only ten minutes — to explain to the accused why he was being executed.

At this time, the second slaughter in Trochenbrot-Ignatovka had just taken place. Trochenbrot-Ignatovka was totally and finally obliterated on Yom Kippur day, 1942. The murderers knew that on that holy day the Jews would get together, so that's when they surrounded them. The skilled craftsmen and their families had been spared during the first slaughter. The Ukrainian nationalist police surrounded these unfortunate Jews, and the Germans killed them. For example, on such an "operation" there might be a hundred Ukrainians and seven or eight Germans. The Germans were members of the killer squads, the *Einsatzgruppen*, who went from town to town, murdering and butchering the Jews.

So Avram Druker almost begged me; he wanted to take Yuleks alive. He knew exactly how to get into Yuleks's house; he knew all the side entrances and back doors. I finally authorized this operation several months after Yom Kippur. It was cold in the woods, and a wet snow was falling, but we had no calendars, so I can't tell you the exact date.

We moved in and surrounded Yuleks' house (his mill was about seventy or eighty meters from the house). We went into the house carefully but only Yuleks' wife was there, with seven or eight small children. "Where's your husband," we asked. "He went away, on business," she answered. We dressed and spoke in such a way as to make identification impossible, but we were well armed. Several days later we returned to the house and received the same answer. After eight or nine attempts, it became obvious that Yuleks was in hiding. We knew that he had been seen in town during the day. The question was, where was he hiding? He had probably made a tunnel underground, and Avram believed that the tunnel went from the house to the mill. There was only one thing left to do. I said to Avram, "We can't return here any more. He'll tip off the Germans. We're going to set fire to the mill and the house." He answered, "When I see the house and mill burning with Yuleks in the flames, that will be the greatest pleasure of my seventeen years." The majority of my men said we should burn everything, children and all. Three of us said no — and we refused to give in. After an hour's discussion, we finally prevailed. The children were obviously innocent. How could we kill them? Did we want to become just like the German and Ukrainian butchers we were fighting? The wife must have had bloody hands, but how could we leave the children motherless? So we led the wife and children out of the house, closed the doors and the doors of the mill, and prepared the site for burning. Druker begged

[41]

to be the one to set it on fire. He had poured some gasoline around, and he set it burning from all four sides. For an hour we waited on the edge of the forest, 200 meters from the house and mill (the whole area was surrounded by forests), and we watched the raging fire. Then we moved off, and from fifteen kilometers we could still see the blazing fire. We later learned that Yuleks had suffocated in the fire.

Avram Druker was with us for another four months before he fell in a heavy battle with German police. We had prepared an ambush. We knew that at a certain time two wagons with police were going by on a certain road. So we hid on both sides of the road. We believed that there would be four, or at the very most six, men against us. They always traveled in a two plus two, or three plus three formation. It turned out that there were seven plus seven — fourteen heavily armed police, who had much more formidable arms than we had. They had to drive out of the forest and straight into the village. We had stationed ourselves near the village. In the woods they were always very much on guard. Experience, of which we had a great deal by now, had taught us that they felt more at ease and confident when they left the forest behind them and could already see the village.

So they were fourteen, and we were four or five. Although we had figured it out completely, those extra numbers had been a bad miscalculation. The fight lasted a full hour. One of their wagons was able to gain the cover of the trees, and there the murderers jumped out, and the battle followed. We captured six rifles but Avram Druker fell in this battle. Despite his severe wounds he lived for an hour, and said to us, "Boys, maybe somebody from my family will survive. If you run into them, tell them that Avram Druker did whatever he could." Avram Druker came from Ignatovka, near Trochenbrot; he was seventeen, no more than that. I have related

[42]

only three operations in which he participated, although he took part in more than twenty. The ones I have told will remain etched in my memory for the rest of my life.

Most of the time we had no trouble moving around. However, on certain occasions, a few hours after we moved to a new site, we were almost surrounded by Germans. (Luckily, we always prepared escape routes.) I thought: We moved around so quietly — how did the Germans know? Then I figured it out. It must be the forest ranger. When we passed him we used to pretend we didn't see him, and he pretended he didn't see us. So we captured this forest ranger and got the truth from him; it was as I had suspected. We paid him back for his interest in us, and we paid another ranger back too. After that, when we moved into an area, the other forest rangers would seek *us* out, looking for a deal. They begged, "We won't squeal. Please, don't be hard on us!" That's the power of force. In that world nothing else mattered.

I want to tell you about Yitzhak der Milchiger (Yitzhak the dairyman) who used the Ukrainian alias Ivan Yakimchuk. At the beginning of our forest existence we had very few arms, and our daily topic of conversation was how to get more. Where do you get them? How do you get them? We didn't have much fighting experience; we didn't have strategies worked out then. One day Yitzhak came to me and told me that he had two good friends from prewar days who lived ten kilometers away. These fellows would help our group by getting us arms and other things. I suggested sending two men to go with Yitzhak, but he insisted on going alone. I discussed it with Kalman Klein, and we agreed to let him go. He was to return the next day.

Seven days passed, and Yitzhak did not come back. Everybody loved him greatly — in every difficult situation he pulled us through. He spoke Ukrainian very well, and when he put on a Ukrainian shirt and went into an Ukrainian village or hamlet, nobody could recognize him as a Jew. We had acquaintances in almost every village. Fearing the worst, we were preparing to send several men to find out what had happened when he returned to us, bringing two rifles and two young men with bound hands.

When he told us how he had captured them, I was angry with him — very angry. I shouted, "We sent you for guns. Why did you bring prisoners? It could have been a disaster, not only for you but for our whole group! You were sent for rifles, not men!" Yitzhak answered me. He knew what I meant, but he was sure that if he had told me that he wanted to capture the two murderers I wouldn't have let him do it alone. And he particularly and specially wanted to do it himself. Kalman Klein interceded for him. "Nahum, forgive him. It happened. He's back in one piece and he's okay, we ought to go along with it." I gave in, but in a more organized, official partisan group, like Medvedev's group (which I was in later), Yitzhak probably would have been kicked out for that kind of behavior.

When things calmed down, we heard Yitzhak's story. He explained that when he went into the village and checked the house, only one of the men was there. Keeping out of sight, he waited several days until the other came too, from Kolki. That night, when both had gone to sleep, Yitzhak opened the window and moved in very quietly. The windows were accessible, because it was a village hut, built low to the ground. Yitzhak saw that their two rifles were near their beds. Grabbing them, he woke the two men with his revolver. (Yitzhak hadn't taken a rifle with him — only a revolver. He wanted it that way.) He moved two or three meters away from them, ordered them to get dressed, and made them both come over with their hands up, on the back of their necks. Yitzhak bound first one and then the other. He forced them into the forest and returned to us with them.

These two Ukrainian nationalists — Banderovtsy — had been, in prewar days, in the Komsomol (Communist Youth Club) with Yitzhak. (Only at this point did I learn that Yitzhak had been in the Komsomol.) Yitzhak knew these two very well, as they often met at meetings. I don't know how to tell you about the crimes of these two. It took two full days to interrogate them and get the picture of what they had done!

In every village, wherever there was a massacre of Jews, these two picked out the nicest Jewish girls — 15, 16, 17, 18, and 19 years old girls — and they kept them several days, raped them repeatedly, and forced their perversions on the innocent girls. After all these terrible things, they took thick sharpened stakes and drove them up the girls' vaginas — drove the stakes in until the girls died. I am sure that even in the tenth century, 1000 years ago, there was not such sadism. And, they committed many other crimes — it's hard to explain it to you. I don't even want to remember such sadistic activities — I've spent the last thirty years trying to forget them. What they did to old people, infants, small children — ah! ah!

When my boys heard this, I could hardly control them — they wanted to rip those two bandits to pieces immediately. But I didn't want to do that. I said, "No, they are our prisoners. They must know why they are being killed. Their crimes must be explained to them." At that time I didn't speak Ukrainian well; I spoke Polish, but all of them could speak Polish because they had gone to Polish schools. So I explained to those two bandits. It took forty minutes to go into every crime for which they were about to die. There were different opinions about what kind of death they should have, but Kalman and I decided not to proceed in a sadistic way. We shot them, just as a criminal is shot for the worst crime. We "appropriated" their two rifles and many bullets. These two were brought to justice because of Yitzhak.

After five or six months I began to appreciate what military and personal talents this Yitzhak had! He used to disguise himself and go into many villages. He had the official right to move around like that. My boys didn't know about it, but he had an official pass from the Germans. We took this pass when we destroyed the military dairy in Trostyanets. In the office there we had found blank passes. Yitzhak had beautiful handwriting, so he forged the proper signature and stamped it with the official stamp. This pass gave him the right to visit all the villages in order to collect milk for the factory. Only Kalman and I knew about this pass.

One day Yitzhak came to see me about a serious matter. There was a very big church in a town about seven kilometers from our position. People from the neighboring villages without churches came to worship there. Yitzhak explained that one of the chief area leaders of the Ukrainian nationalist collaborators, Panchinko, went to that church regularly. Panchinko had been born near Lutsk. When the Russians had come into the western Ukraine he had run to Germany, but in 1941, when the Germans came back to that area, he returned with them. They made him the leader of the whole area. Kalman and I discussed the situation. We thought it through carefully, and we agreed that Yitzhak had to go every Sunday to that church.

So Yitzhak became "devout." My boys knew that he used to leave for church services and return four or five hours later. They used to laugh at him. They said; "You didn't want to go to the synagogue, so now you have to go to church — that's your punishment!" Yitzhak had learned to pray better than a

[46]

Christian; he used to cross himself and go through all the ceremonies.

After a while Yitzhak proposed to me that he kill Panchinko in church. I didn't agree to that. We didn't know very much about what other dangerous people might be in that church. I called Kalman over and made him understand that it wasn't a good idea because Yitzhak would die there for this. That Yitzhak should die because of Panchinko — it just wasn't worth it! So we rejected the plan, and we explained to Yitzhak that a different type of attack, outside the church and its environs, was called for.

The following Sunday Yitzhak again came to me and said he had a plan to take Panchinko alive. "Listen," I asked him, "are you going to give me a cock-and-bull story like the one about the two boys and the rifles, and then go ahead and do what you want anyhow?" He said; "No. I'm not up to any such deception. We must discuss my plan and check every detail." So we planned together. Yitzhak told me that he had mentioned Shoykhet to Panchinko. Before the war, Shoykhet had a very big textile store in Lutsk. He was a very wealthy Jew who had manufactured fabrics; and Panchinko had known him well. Yitzhak told Panchinko that he knew Shoykhet was living in the forest in a bunker, where he had salted away all his wealth. Yitzhak suggested that Shoykhet could be quietly disposed of and all his wealth "confiscated." Panchinko, on hearing this, became all ears. He asked, "You know exactly where Shoykhet and his bunker are?" Yitzhak said, "Yes!" Panchinko replied, "Great! Wonderful!" Yitzhak suggested that they had better take two policemen with them, but Panchinko replied, "What for?" Yitzhak said, "Maybe this *Zhid** is armed? Everything is possible!" But Panchinko laughed: "A *Zhid* with arms? Ah, Jews can't shoot. Ha! Ha!" And he continued, using Yitzhak's alias, "Ivan, listen to me.

* Derogatory term for Jew.

[47]

Nobody should know about this — only you and me, or we'll have to start dividing the pie many ways. Next Sunday, after church services, we'll drive over to that forest and take care of this matter."

Yitzhak told me about this and his plan to capture Panchinko. My men made various suggestions. One said that we should seize him right at the beginning and take him with force. But I had an idea. I told Yitzhak: "If you said that Shoykhet is in a bunker, then let's build a bunker! It should be visible from as far away as possible, and a distant viewer should think there's somebody there. When you approach with Panchinko, we're going to retreat a couple of hundred meters to the side. When Panchinko tries to open the bunker, you'll give him a hard blow. Then you'll whistle, and we'll come."

We knew more or less, within half an hour either way, the time Panchinko would approach the bunker. Yitzhak said he would be driving. As the time approached, I put two observers near the road to let us know when Panchinko and Yitzhak were really coming. From afar we saw Panchinko and Yitzhak on two horses, so we moved off a distance of 200 meters. Panchinko could see there was a bunker there. He got off the horse and asked, "This is the bunker?" Yitzhak answered affirmatively, so Panchinko asked, "How do you open it?" Yitzhak said, "There's a door there." And as Panchinko bent down he gave him a big blow to the head, which knocked him unconscious. Yitzhak grabbed Panchinko's revolver and whistled to us. When we joined them, Panchinko was still out cold. It took ten to fifteen minutes till he came to himself. He saw so many of our men around, he quickly understood into whose hands he had fallen. We held Panchinko for several days. A whole book could be written from interrogation. What crimes this beast committed!

[48]

Panchinko was an organizer of Jewish labor for the Germans. He formed factories staffed with Jewish tailors, shoemakers, and so on. He worked them hard for a year or so, and then they were killed. During this year Panchinko exploited them; that's why he didn't want them killed immediately. He gave them absolutely impossible work quotas, and then he brutally beat those who fell short. He didn't hit them himself; he had his men do the beating on his express orders. If the workers filled the quota, he ordered beatings anyhow, till the workers fell unconcious. Panchinko accepted "gifts" from the workers too. The tailor or shoemaker could bring his wife and children with him, so Panchinko took the best women and nicest girls and changed every day. This took place near Lutsk, and it went on till these unfortunate Jews were liquidated. It was heart-rending just to hear about these Jews.

One of my men, Schwartz, gave a yell. "God! How can we allow such a thing — that so much innocent Jewish blood should be spilled, so many guiltless Jewish souls should be drowned in their own blood?" Some of my men started to cry. Kalman Klein said, "We have to take revenge, even more revenge than before!" After Schwartz's exclamation, we thought about the kind of death we should give this Panchinko beast. Everybody gave his opinion. The majority said we should hang him on a tree with his head down, and in his pocket we should put a piece of paper on which we would write the basic facts of why he had been executed. I disagreed with that opinion. I always had a different approach to such matter. But this time even Kalman Klein was with the majority, not with me. I said, "Why do that? He came to rob Shoykhet's wealth from this bunker, so I feel that we should tie his feet and his hands, and we should put him into the bunker. And let him stay there until he dies. All his yelling would be useless because the bunker was so well dug in that nobody would hear a thing.

It was very hard for me to talk them into it. They said, "We can't stick around here very long." But I promised them we would stay until we were sure he was dead. I figured that this was a better death for him. "Let him feel and see and know how Jews feel lying buried alive in such bunkers. Let him feel and see how good life is there; let him have a taste of that kind of life!" And that's what we did. We tied him up and put him in the bunker. I had figured that his dying would take four days, but it took a much longer time — more than a week. We used to keep moving, but this time we had to wait eleven or twelve days. Only then did my boys learn why Yitzhak had gone to church regularly; he hadn't gone there as a sightseer. Only then did they learn what Yitzhak was capable of.

It usually took us several hours to cross from one forest to another, and we always followed a system. First, we sent two reconnaissance men to look the area over. One would come back, give the all-clear signal, and then we would move forward. Whenever our group stood still we would have two or three men sweeping our perimeter, on reconnaissance duty. Once one man returned from the perimeter area and said that he had heard something moving in the forest. So we sent another man; he lay in the forest for about half an hour, and then he returned and said, "Yes, I did hear something too. Somebody or something is moving out there!" So I went out with several men. Remember sound carries very clearly in the forest. You can hear even a twig cracking a kilometer away. And we did hear. Something *was* going on out there. We didn't know what or who it was — it could have been Ukrainian nationalists. Three men had to move in closer and find out.

We closed in very, very cautiously. When we came close to the source of the sound, we saw that a hole had been dug in the ground, one meter deep and lined with moss. Three people were lying there, completely naked as the day they were born. We saw immediately that these were Jews. As we approached closer, those three people became terribly frightened. The woman started to rip chunks of hair from her head. She started to beg, "Please don't kill us! Okay, kill us, but spare the boy! Please! Please!" I tried to answer, "What are you yelling for? We're also Jews!" It didn't help. No explanation could calm them — they were hysterical. The man was pulling his beard, ripping chunks out of it, the woman was pulling her hair out. I continued to try to calm them. I repeated a dozen times, "We are Jews, just as you are." We were hugging them, calming them, reassuring them. They still wouldn't believe us! They were paralyzed at the sight of our rifles.

It took a good twenty minutes until we could convince them that we were Jews. The son was the first to understand. He calmed the mother and father. After some time, we pieced together what had happened. They came from Trostyanets and they had escaped from a massacre. They had already been undressed for the slaughter — that's why they were naked. They had had two daughters as well as this son — three children in all. The man, his wife, and their son had managed to escape, running into the woods. There they dug a hole in which they huddled together. The father, at night, used to sneak over to a pigsty in a nearby hamlet to steal the rotten food from the pigs. They also ate berries from the forest, bark, leaves — that's how they were existing. When we found them, they had been living like that for many weeks. When they stole food from the pigs it went unnoticed, but stealing clothes from a yard would be immediately noticed, and the friendly peasants would organize a posse; so these terrified Jews did not try to get clothes. It was too risky.

There were tears in every eye when my boys saw and heard. They immediately insisted on giving these unfortunates their clothes — pants, shirts, jackets. First they covered them, and then they dressed them. Everybody was competing to dress them with his clothes. Because of them we remained in that area for several weeks, which we usually didn't do. The father, in prewar days, had been in the shoe trade; he supplied shoemakers with heels, soles, and so on. He explained to us which Ukrainian had seized his tools and stock. We settled up with that thief. The mother and father begged us to take the boy into our group. We would have taken him with us but for one problem — his feet had started to rot. His toes were in atrocious condition — he could hardly walk, even with improvised crutches. We went to the nearest village and "appropriated" fats — lard, cow fat, and chicken fat — and we brought it to him to rub on his feet. We couldn't take his parents with us at all. We built a solid shelter for them and left them food for eight or nine months. The father had named a Banderovets (Ukrainian nationalist) who had robbed Jews; this crook had killed a pig and smoked it — it could last a year in that condition. We brought the pig to these unfortunates; we brought full barrels of food to them and left them well supplied. But whether they survived I cannot say.

There were other incidents like that, but this one — the three of them lying there naked and shrieking hysterically — I can never forget!

I mentioned Schwartz, one of my boys, earlier. After the Panchinko affair, he complained to me, "Why didn't you send me with Yitzhak? I can also speak Ukrainian. I could have helped!" I explained to him, "Schwartz, what you can

[52]

do on the battlefield Yitzhak can't do as well, and what Yitzhak can do I cannot do as well. Every person has his special talent." And Yitzhak agreed, "It's true, Schwartz. What you can do well, I can't do as well." Schwartz was eager to avenge his dead, and yet he was a refined boy. He came from an impoverished home and had completed only the fourth grade of primary school, but he was born a refined person — it was in his blood.

There's a lot to say about Schwartz. He came to us from the Trochenbrot area when he was 16 years old. His father was a leatherworker, an employee. There were five children in the house, and they lived in poverty because there wasn't enough work to keep his father employed for a whole year. Schwartz had always comforted his parents. He had told them that when he would grow up, he would earn and contribute his earnings to the family. Things would improve. But, unfortunately, when Schwartz turned 16, the Germans were already in Trochenbrot.

He came to us without arms. He obtained his first rifle in a battle with the nationalists at Juravyem, a hamlet. Until then, Schwartz, lacking a gun, used a big knife as his weapon. In that battle he obtained his rifle, and there I saw what kind of man this was, what heroism he was capable of. But there was much more to him than that.

After every mission and battle, we used to sit around a small fire. The boys used to like to rehash the engagement — whether our method was right, how we might have modified it, and so forth. Schwartz didn't like this type of conversation. He always went off by himself and lay down a few meters away from the fire. He would put his hands under his head and lie there for hours, staring at the sky, never saying a word to anybody. Some of my boys came over to me and asked me whether Schwartz was "all there," whether he wasn't mentally disturbed. I spoke to Schwartz a number of times, and I saw that he was not mentally ill; he was a serious and sensitive boy who was taking to heart the terrible things he had seen. I begged my boys, "Listen, when he lies down like that, don't bother him. Don't tease him. Let him live." I understood that the German atrocities were affecting him greatly. He often spoke about his brothers and sisters to me; he evidently could not recover so rapidly from what happened.

After some time, however, I, too, became uneasy about what could be happening to the boy. He had stopped talking altogether. I then reversed my earlier position and told my boys, "He's our responsibility. When you come back after a mission, include him. Make him feel that he's a part of the group." I knew what a warm and sensitive human being was lurking behind the silence. One day, Schwartz came to see me with a request. "I need notebooks and pencils." I asked, "For what?" He explained, "Everything we saw, everything that has gone on, everything we are doing *must* be preserved, *must* be written down. I want to write a log book, a group history, and every day entries should be made in this book." At first, I hesitated, and many of the boys said, "Ah, now is not the time for that! Now is the time to take revenge and not to scribble in notebooks." But Kalman Klein spoke up. "Especially now, when we are avenging our brothers, sisters, and parents, we should be writing it down and preserving it. I agree with Schwartz." I concluded by agreeing with Kalman, and I said that writing it down would be a part of our revenge-taking. We *had* to do it. And we would do it.

So I gathered all the boys together. Of course, nobody had pencil or paper. So I said, "Schwartz, as soon as we get a chance we'll get your 'arms' — pencils and notebooks." Unfortunately in our next several battles, we took rifles and other things, but we never came across any pencils or notebooks. And soon, Schwartz was coming to me every day, asking when he would get them. Finally, I called Yitzhak and told him what we needed. "I know you get around a lot," I said. "Get those notebooks and pencils somewhere!"

After several days, the ever-industrious and resourceful Yitzhak came to me with a proposition. Four kolometers from Tsuman there was a recruiting office, which sent people to Germany for munitions work. This place was full of notebooks. So Yitzhak proposed that we kill two birds with one stone. We could get notebooks and pencils for Schwartz, and at the same time we could destroy that office and disrupt their shipping of people to Germany for their war effort. I asked Yitzhak, "How many people are there in that office?" He said, "Not many." I asked him again. "Go and find out *exactly* how many people there are in that office." After several days, he returned and reported that there were three or four Germans, several Ukrainian nationalist police, and two female typists.

I called Kalman in, and we made a plan. I wanted to take our whole group on this operation, but Kalman said five or six men would be enough. Either Kalman or I had to remain behind, because we were awaiting the arrival of one of Yitzhak's contacts with important news. So I stayed, and Kalman went with six men. They returned the next day with a sack full of pencils and notebooks, and the joy on Schwartz's face was evident — it was like a new face! If he wrote for ten years he couldn't use them all. The boys told me how Schwartz had fought like a lion. It had been a well-organized, lightning attack. From all the doors and windows they had stormed in at the same time, so that no alarm could be given. But Schwartz had jumped into the German office first — he didn't even shoot. He jumped on one German and bit through his throat. The whole engagement lasted only five minutes; my boys cleaned the whole place out. I was curious. "Schwartz," I asked him, "you had a rifle on this mission. At the beginning, when you first joined us, you lacked a rifle, but now we have more rifles than men. Why didn't you use your rifle?" He answered, simply, "It was a pity to waste a bullet on such animals."

Every day thereafter Schwartz would go off by himself to note everything down. Even those boys who, at the beginning had laughed at him and considered him "off" now respected him greatly. When they saw him writing there, on the side, nobody dared go near him. He wrote like that for several months. He remembered what had happened many months before, and he wrote it all down. He kept watch over his notebooks with the same care that he gave to his rifle.

One day Schwartz came to me and said, "First I asked for notebooks and pencils. Now, I have to ask you for one more thing. Where should we put these notebooks? We don't know which of us will survive. The next generation should receive these notebooks — it will be their heritage." This was indeed a serious matter, and I knew I could not make such a decision alone. I said, "Schwartz, we have to gather the whole group, and everybody has to give an opinion as to where to hide these notebooks. After the war they must fall into the hands of future generations!"

That same evening I called the whole group together, and I explained the problem to them. Many volunteered to keep the notebooks, but I told them, "How can you be sure that you will remain alive? Or that your comrade will remain alive?" Finally, we agreed that the books should be buried under a tree with everybody witnessing the burial. Whoever survived would recover them later. But now Schwartz became stubborn. He said that the notebooks had to be buried in the yard of the Trochenbrot house where he was born. He said he would show us the tree. I suggested that all of our boys should be there, because we didn't know who would survive. So we agreed that, when we were near Trochenbrot, we would all go to bury the notebooks. Trochenbrot was empty, all the houses were wide open, and half the houses had already been dismantled by scavenging Ukrainians, who had carted off everything, even the walls and floors. Houses were destroyed, but the yards remained, and Schwartz was sure he knew exactly which tree grew in his own yard.

Kalman Klein pointed out that these notebooks would rot in the earth; we had to find big jars, and we would put crushed glass in the jars and hide the notebooks in the glass. Even if none of us survived, we were going to write, in Ukrainian, that these jars should be given to a Jewish organization or society.

Unfortunately, the times were such that we couldn't be near Trochenbrot-Ignatovka. These were the last weeks of my group's existence, because the Germans were looking for us relentlessly. Every day we had to move, and move fast. We had been in the forest over a year, so we knew it well, but we couldn't rest — we had to move constantly and rapidly. The Germans knew that the leader of this group was "the watchmaker from Tsuman" — that's what they called me.

After every massacre, ten or twenty percent of the young people escaped. Many were caught immediately, but some made it into the woods. Salt was almost unobtainable then, so the Germans rewarded every Christian who killed a Jew or brought him in alive with half a kilogram of salt. But, for the watchmaker — I learned about this only later — they offered a special bounty. They announced in Tsuman that anybody who knew where the watchmaker was and could show them would get two kilograms of salt. Anybody who could have brought me in alive would have received five kilograms of salt. I saw the "wanted" poster for me later, when I was with Felyuk's group, and a friend brought the poster in after a mission.

So we kept moving until the Germans surrounded us completely. My group no longer consisted of eighteen men — we were down to eight. Our last fight with the Germans wasn't a battle of equals — we were outnumbered and outgunned. We had rifles and revolvers, and they had submachine guns, machine guns, and more. The battle started at six in the morning, when they surrounded us, and it continued for about five hours. They were able to split us up into small groups of two or three men each, so I had no contact with my men. I couldn't suggest a plan; I could no longer give orders. I believe, to this day, that they could have killed us all immediately, but they wanted to capture several of us alive for interrogation.

So they had driven wedges between us, and we lost contact with each other. They pushed me to a riverbank. Wet snow was falling then; it was very cold. I now faced what could hardly even be called a "choice": I could surrender alive or jump, clothes and all, into the river, called the Styr. I had nobody alive near me any more. The Styr is a big, fast-flowing river, and, since it wasn't summer any longer, I was dressed fairly heavily. But it was surely better in the river than in the Germans' hands, so I jumped in with my rifle. I had been born near a big river, the Warta was 200 meters from my parents' house. It is one of the biggest rivers in Poland (the Warta and the Vistula are mentioned in the Polish national anthem), and I practically lived in the water. I was an excellent swimmer. The Germans were sure that I would swim, at most, several hundred meters, and I would then have to come out. How could anybody swim in that freezing, fast-flowing water? So, for several kilometers, they ran along the river bank with the idea of taking me alive. They shot all around me. I kept rising and submerging in the water. They could have shot me, but, it would seem, they wanted to capture me alive. So they ran along the shore for some distance, but then they couldn't follow very well because there were muddy marshlands along the shoreline. At that point they wanted to kill me, but it was too late. The marshes prevented them from moving in. I swam for another one and a half kilometers, rising and submerging in the water, when I realized that they couldn't see me well anymore because the river was no longer straight — it turned right and then left.

I can't tell you how far I swam. I swam with blind desperation. When I was far enough away, and I saw that they couldn't get at me, I swam over to the other shore and dragged myself onto the riverbank. I was half dead — no, 90 percent dead. I went five meters up the riverbank, and then I couldn't move a muscle. I must have been unconscious on the ground for about half an hour. When I regained consciousness, I had to get undressed completely and wring out my soaking clothes. Before I did that, however, I used branches and leaves to dry out every single part of my drenched pistol. Everything else was unimportant. I had to make sure that the pistol was operating. Once it was operating, then I could worry about other things. Because without the pistol, there would be nothing else to worry about. I knew that as long as it worked, I could get new clothing. My revolver was my treasure, my wealth. It was worth more than diamonds, gold, or rubies, especially since I had lost my rifle in the water.

I had no idea where I was, which was worse than everything else. I saw a light in the distance, so I went in that direction. I was as naked as the day I was born. I had my wet clothing, or what was left of it (I had discarded some in the water to make swimming easier) in one hand, and my revolver in the other hand. I had grown a beard — I must have looked quite a sight! The hut was about six kilometers away. I approached it cautiously and looked through the window to make sure that the inhabitants were elderly. I was exhausted, and I lacked my rifle. It was cold, and the evening had set in. I entered the hut and let them see the revoler immediately. They understood. They had a Russian-style stove so I used it to dry my clothes. They told me where the hut was located, so I could orient myself.

In my group, we had made an agreement among ourselves that, in the event of an emergency, if something should happen, we would meet at a certain place. This meeting place was a thick tree near the forest ranger tower where we had obtained our first gun (the forest rangers were no longer there — they had abandoned their posts). We were supposed to wait at this meeting place for several days, and if nobody else showed up, we were supposed to leave a note as to our whereabouts for whoever might show up later. We always left a pencil and a piece of paper hidden there. It was ten days before I could get to that meeting place, and there I met my friend, Kalman Klein, and another fellow, a youngster. We three were all that was left of my group of eighteen. In the last battle, Schwartz had been killed and his notebooks lost. Perhaps they fell into German hands and are in Germn archives somewhere. Maybe the Germans tore up the notebooks, or burned them? We'll probably never know. Schwartz never had the opportunity to bury his precious notebooks.

I must tell you that all of my men fell as heroes. Perhaps, for historians, what they accomplished was of no importance, but for me and my conscience their deeds shine with greatness. They weren't content to spend one day, or sleep one night, without having done something against the enemy. As long as they felt they could do something, as long as they felt that a crime cried out for revenge, they pushed me and themselves to take revenge. Many times I counseled patience, but they would insist. I have singled out a few in these pages, but everyone of them had a brave record and accomplished great things! It pains me that I don't remember all these others' names — but so many years have passed, and so much has happened. I remember how Kalman Klein fought valorously; there was a Shuster, and there was a boy called Avraimale. Avraimale fought like a real tiger! Extraordinary! Little Avraimale — I can see his eager face before my eyes even now!

Avraimale had camouflaged himself in the branches of a tree. We knew that, at a certain time, a policeman would use the road to go from one village to another. Just as he drove into the forest, Avraimale jumped on him, bit through his throat, and took his gun. What heroism! We didn't order him to do that. He explained that he had known that this policeman had murdered his sister. We couldn't get at this policeman in the village, so Avraimale came up with the ambush plan.

My seventeen Jewish boys, in that one year of action, accomplished a *very* great deal. Our enemies, who spilled our innocent blood, did their dastardly deeds, but my boys did whatever they could do against them. My men didn't want to sleep or hide. They fought — and they fell — heroically!

So my group met its end in combat — my boys would have wanted it that way. I would have known nothing more about our final hours except for a remarkable coincidence. In 1945, after the war, I was sent, with twenty partisans, to Kiev. In Kiev I went to work at my trade as a watchmaker. I became friendly with the watchmakers working near me. Among them were the Ratz brothers, who helped me very much with parts for watches.

Once, when I needed a part for a watch, I went into Ratz's workplace, and, as I was talking to him, I noticed a young Soviet soldier sitting on a stool there. I saw that the soldier was looking at me intently. After I had been chatting for about ten minutes, I glanced at the soldier and saw that his look was even more intent. As I was leaving the shop, he came over to me and said, *"Tovarishch Kommandeer,* * do you recognize me?" When I did not, he said, "I was in your group." "You?" I said, and, as I looked at him carefully, I started to remember . . . and remember. "You are . . . you are . . ." As he spoke he started to stammer a little. "Ah, you are my Yossele!" I said. "How do you come here? How did you survive? Why didn't you leave a note afterwards at the meeting place? We said that everyone of us who survived was to meet there and write down where he was and what he was doing." At my words, he started to cry. He took off his tunic, ripped off his undershirt, and he showed me, on his right side, a massive scar under his breast. In the forest he had worn tattered rags and was thin as a stick. Now he was well-fed, in uniform.

He explained to me that in our last fight, when we were surrounded by the Germans, he had been injured. So he dragged himself on his hands and knees into some thick bushes. He was lying there for an hour, or an hour and a half, and in a moment of consciousness he ripped off his shirt and blocked the wound where the bullet had entered. When the Germans surrounded us, they brought with them a considerable number of peasants from the neighboring

* Comrade commander.

[62]

villages to assist them. You could travel there only with horses and carts, not with cars or trucks. While Yossele was lying there in the thicket, a peasant poked around and noticed him. He called Yossele by his name, because in the peasant's village, four or five kilometers from Trochenbrot, there had been one Jewish family — Yossele's family. They had had a general store there. The peasants from the surrounding area knew this one Jewish family very well.

When the peasant saw Yossele, he took leaves and grass and covered him, and he said, "You lie here; I'll return tomorrow, and I'll see what I can do for you." So Yossele lay there all night. The next day, in the early morning, when the farmer came, Yossele was half dead. He put Yossele in a cart and brought him to his house. Yossele was hardly conscious during the whole ride. The peasant kept Yossele in his house for several months.

From one hundred of these peasants you would, if you were lucky, find two or three such people. It was Yossele's luck that he fell into the hands of one of these two or three. After several months, Yossele regained his health. He told me that he did go to our meeting place, and there he saw that Kalman and I had remained alive. He didn't even tell the farmer where he was going when he set out for that thick three. So he knew that we were alive, but he didn't know where we were. He only knew what the note we had left told him: that we had gone to look for the Ukrainian group that had been operating in our area. At that time, we didn't even know the name of the group's leader.

The farmer told Yossele that the Germans had collected the dead bodies of our boys. They piled these bodies into wagons and took them to Tsuman. They gathered all the people of Tsuman together and said, "Look at these corpses carefully! Is the watchmaker among the dead?" The townspeople said, "No, we don't see him among these dead." Yossele told me that the farmer had mentioned the bounty on my head. When the Germans saw that they hadn't captured me, they printed special posters and put a price on my head, dead or alive. When Yossele told me that, he started to cry. I hugged him; only then did we embrace. I told him about Kalman Klein. I also told him how I came to join the Ukrainian group under the command of Aleksandr Fyodorovich Felyuk.

I invited Yossele to my room, but he couldn't come because he only had a two hour pass. His division was leaving that day for Manchuria, near the Japanese border. The war had ended in Europe, and the Russians were moving against Japan. So I walked him back to the train, and I remained with him until it left. He gave me his word that when he got to his destination he would write. I gave him my address, and we agreed that when he was demobilized at the end of the war, he would join me in Kiev. I told him that I would wait for him; I would stay in Kiev for six months after hostilities ceased waiting for him. But I waited nine months, and I received no letters; nor did he come. He went away, and I never heard from him again.

So, after the last battle of my group, only three of us found our way to the meeting place: Kalman, the young boy from Trochenbrot-Ignatovka, and I. We knew that we were finished — with three men you can't accomplish anything. We had to link up with a larger group. We determined, therefore, to find an antifascist Ukrainian group we knew of, which had done great things against the Germans and the anti-Semitic Ukrainian nationalists. We searched for this group for many months.

My own Jewish group was not written into the official Soviet archives. I asked for its inclusion there many times,

[64]

but I was unsuccessful. My partisan activities were recognized only from the moment I joined Felyuk's group. Whatever came before didn't count for the Soviets, although they knew all about it in great detail, as was evident from the interrogation I received later when I joined the official Soviet partisans.

PART TWO

We used to send the young boy who was with us out to various villages and hamlets. He spoke Ukrainian very well (Kalman and I were foreigners), and we hoped he would be able to find the large Ukrainian antifascist group for us. In May of 1942 he returned to us from a Ukrainian village, Klopochin, four kilometers from Trochenbrot with the news that Aleksandr Fyodorovich Felyuk was the leader of that group. I mention Felyuk's name with great pride. He is worthy of being remembered — the world should have more of such rare and humane people. So we sent our boy out with orders that he must leave no stone unturned — he *must* find out where and how we could make contact with Felyuk's group.

He returned after a short while and told us that he had made contact with Felyuk. He had actually seen him, and Felyuk said that he had heard of us and wanted to see us. So we agreed on a place and a time, and we met Felyuk fifteen kilometers from Trochenbrot. We came rather empty-handed; I had a pistol, Kalman Klein had a pistol, and the boy had nothing. I couldn't speak Ukrainian at that time, although I had been a year in the Ukrainian forest by then. However, I understood the language well.

We came to the appointed place, and a tall, thin fellow came over to me. He carried a rifle and a compass and wore a Russian military-type shirt. He shook hands with me and said, "I have heard of you; I really wanted to meet you. I wanted to make contact with you, but I couldn't." I answered him, "We're just a remnant now. Once we were many." He replied, "I heard many good things about your group — you accomplished a great deal! I sent my men out to look for you, but you moved around too rapidly — you really moved fast! I could take you into my group, but we have one un-breakable rule here: every member of our group must have his own rifle. You lost your rifle in a battle from which nobody could emerge alive — I *know* no ordinary human being could have come out alive from such a battle." And he put his hand on my shoulder, and he said, "I believe that you will get a rifle in battle."

I said, "I agree to every order. I'm no longer the com-mander; you are my commander now, and I will follow your orders." So Felyuk asked me whether I knew Trochenbrot. I said, "Of course, I worked there." Then he asked, "Do you know that only Jews were living there?" I said, "Yes." He continued, "There are no longer any Jews in Trochenbrot. All the houses are empty. A gendarmerie major and seven policemen are stationed there. Across the road from where the post office was, there's a yard. When the Soviet soldiers retreated, they buried rifles and bullets there. That's where you can get a rifle. If you agree to go on this mission and dig up the cache, you can join us." I agreed.

Felyuk then said, "Take your friend with you. I'll give you, as a guide, a Jew who used to live near that yard. He's in my group, and he'll show you exactly where the rifles are buried. That's where you'll get your rifle. Prepare a plan, and tell me what it is when you're ready." He gave me a 13-year-old boy as a guide. I knew where the post office had been located, but I didn't know the yard well. We were carefully briefed. Of the seven policemen stationed there, three patrolled the yards, three were inside, and one was asleep.

[70]

Every Jew in Trochenbrot used to have his own plot in the yard, and he used to fence it in with a wire fence. The forest surrounded Trochenbrot very snugly; it began 200 meters from one side of the village and continued 200 meters from the other side of the village. The village was, in effect, in a clearing in the woods. We moved from the forest into the yard to a plot adjoining our target, and the boy showed us exactly where he thought the cache had been buried. Before we moved in on the exact place, we made an agreement: Near Trochenbrot there was a small Jewish hamlet, Shelish, that once contained forty or fifty Jewish families. Near this hamlet there was a dump for wrecked Russian tanks. We agreed that, whatever might happen, any survivor must wait for the others for three days near that dump. We agreed to whistle in a certain way as an identifying signal.

When we came to the place that the guide had indicated to us, we started to dig. There was nothing there. Absolutely nothing! So then the boy said, "Well, perhaps it's over there." We dug and again found nothing. The time was passing. The boy said, "Let's forget it for now. We'll come back some other time." "Oh, no!" I said. "We *have* to find the rifles *now*. The gendarmes will see that somebody was digging here, and they'll be on their guard. It's now or never!" We knew that without the rifles we were worthless — we'd be finished. The boy then said that the rifles might be hidden in the attic of the nearest house. The attic was covered with straw, and in those piles of straw there might be rifles hidden.

We took a ladder from another house. All the Jews from the village had been slaughtered. The houses stood gaping, empty. Only the gendarmerie was there. In the side of the house there was a little door leading into the attic. We put the ladder up against the side of the house, and I told Kalman and the boy to move off some small distance while I climbed into the attic and started to search. The attic had wooden beams; straw was wrapped around the beams. Searching in this straw, I found silver goblets that unfortunate Jews had hidden there. I found Jewish family records — marriage contracts and the like. Just before I was to go down I found seven bayonets. In half an hour of frantic searching, that was all I was able to find of any military use.

I came down with the seven bayonets and went back to our meeting place. The boy wanted to leave because it was nearly dawn, but I wouldn't hear of it. I was almost shouting. *"We can't leave here without rifles."* Reluctantly, the boy suggested a neighboring plot. He measured six meters, and we started to dig. Nothing! We tried another place he indicated, and we hit something hard. When I saw what it was, I gave a shout, "Bullets!" The police must have heard my enthusiastic exclamation. I had taken off my jacket, which we filled with bullets. We figured that, with the bullets there, the rifles must be nearby.

The night was still so dark that we failed to notice that the Ukrainian police had quietly moved in on us. They suddenly opened fire. They were firing steadily, as we three took off for the forest. I ran 200 meters and fell into a ditch. When I stood up two policemen seized me. I tried to pull away. I was young and strong, but I couldn't break loose. A third policeman, carrying a lamp, came over. He held the lamp up to my face, looked at me, and with a laugh he said, "Ah, I know him — he's the watchmaker from Tsuman." In 1940 I had worked in Tsuman, and this area we were now in was under Tsuman's jurisdiction. The policeman continued, "What are you doing here?" I had an idea — if I told them something they might free my hands — then I might have a chance. So I said, "In the forest I ran into the Jew who used to live in this house, and he told me that he had buried gold here. So we made a deal — we would share the gold fifty-fifty if I would dig it up." One guard said, "Oh, yes, I know that rotten Jew he's talking about."

As I was explaining, another policeman called out, "Hey, boys, hold him tight! Come over here!" I tried to pull myself loose from them, because I figured that the game would be up once they went over to the hole and saw what kind of gold I was looking for. While I was writhing about here and there, trying to break loose, I was struck hard in the head with a rifle butt, and I became semi-conscious.

They dragged me over to the bullets we had dug up, and one of them said, "Ah, so this is the kind of gold you were looking for!" And they started to beat me up. The beating lasted a number of minutes. I tried to hit back, but I received some heavy blows to the head and lost consciousness. So, covered with blood as I was, I must have been dragged into the office of the German major. (Those who had captured me were Ukrainian police.) The German officer had a Ukrainian interpreter. This interpreter took a look at me and said, "Dirty Jew! You are dirtying up our earth with your filthy blood!" Blood was pouring from my ears, nose, and mouth; they wiped it up, cursing me all the while. The German major ordered, "Take him to the jail, and bring him back at ten o'clock tomorrow morning."

They took me out of the office, one policeman in front of me, the other just behind me. Both had rifles. I didn't know where they were taking me — I didn't even know what was happening, because I was very groggy. I had received a severe beating, and my mind wasn't working at all. We walked about 200 meters until we came to the "jail." It had once been a small Jewish store. It had shutters and bars on the windows, and a big padlock on the door. One policeman said, "Give me the key." The other replied, "Didn't you bring

[73]

the key?" "No." "Well, neither did I." So the first one said, "You go back and bring the key. I'll guard the prisoner." He would have to go 200–300 meters to get the key, and then he would have to walk the same distance back to us.

At precisely that moment I came to myself — everything became clear to me. I remembered what had happened to me, and I thought about my predicament. What could I do? Resist now, or later? Where could I run if I did manage to escape? A hundred ideas flashed through my mind in one second. Although I had taken a severe beating, I didn't feel the pain yet. Frankly, I was at a loss — I couldn't figure out what I should do.

The guard who remained to watch me placed me against one doorpost of the "jail," while he remained standing near the other doorpost. He asked me if I had a cigarette. I replied that I wasn't a smoker. He started searching in his pockets for a cigarette, found one, and then asked me if I carried matches. I told him that I had no matches. Ideas were starting to crystallize in my mind. Then he put his rifle between his knees and took out some matches. I raised my hand and gave him a terrific punch. His head hit the doorpost, and he fell forward, unconscious, on me. I grabbed his rifle as he fell, pushed him aside, and took off for the woods.

I ran ten meters — no more — and my legs would no longer function. I couldn't get one more step out of them. I thought: What can I do now? Every house or store in Trochenbrot was separated from the next house by five to seven meters. It seemed best to drag myself into the nearest house and stay there, which I did. Every kitchen there had a cold storage cellar for potatoes, onions, and the like. I opened the trapdoor to the cellar, placed the ladder in position, and went down.

Only when I was in the cellar, did I hear "my" policeman

whistle for help. Only then had he regained his senses. All the other policemen ran over to him, and then they headed for the forest, to look for me. It was lucky for me that I hadn't reached the forest; in my condition I would have been hunted down rapidly. The policemen were in the woods for about an hour. I heard shooting, and shortly thereafter I heard them returning. They walked right past my hiding place. And one of them said: "Zhid udral!* Dirty Jew. Filthy Jew bastard!" He addressed another policeman, "I don't envy you now. You're going to get your ass kicked in for this."

I decided it would be better not to move off now; I would wait for the next night. At about noon a local farmer came into the empty house. By this time, I believe that five months had passed since the last remaining Jews had been slaughtered, but Ukrainians were still coming to loot Jewish property. This farmer came as a scavenger, to steal whatever he could find. By now, I had started to feel the pain; blood was dripping from my ears and nose. I could taste blood in my mouth. I was dying of thirst. I had taken the ladder away from the trap door, and I was sitting off to a side, on an upside-down pail. The Ukrainian figured that something might be hidden in the cellar, so he opened the trap door. I prepared the rifle; one shot would bring them all running, but I would at least take this one with me. The scavenger saw that there was no ladder, so he spat out contemptuously. The spit landed right in my face. He grumbled, "The rotten Jews even hid the bloody ladder!" And he went away.

In the evening, I climbed up and went out. I made my way cautiously to our rendezvous point near the smashed tanks. I waited there for ten, fifteen, twenty minutes, but I failed to

* The kike escaped.

[75]

see Kalman and the boy; I wondered if they had been captured too. We had agreed to whistle in a certain way as our signal to each other, but I couldn't whistle because my lips had been split, and my mouth was all swollen. Just when I was about to give up on them, I heard whistling. I tried to whistle back, but what came out was a half whistle, half moan. I was in rotten shape. Kalman and the boy came over; they had escaped, and they were very happy to see me. They looked me over and saw that I had had quite a working over. The important thing was that I still had the policeman's rifle in my hand.

We returned fifteen or sixteen kilometers to the partisans' camp. I could hardly walk. When we came to Felyuk, I wanted to explain to him what had happened. He took one look at me, started to laugh, and put his hand on my shoulder. He said, "You don't have to explain — I know everything. You accomplished more than just obtaining a rifle! You're one hell of a guy! From today on, you're all in my group, and you, Kohn, will be among my right-hand men!" I had been feeling my wounds, and my whole mouth was badly swollen. Felyuk saw that I could hardly talk, but his words, in the middle of the woods, cheered me up immensely. I would be back in the thick of the fight again. I lived only for revenge.

After these words, Felyuk introduced me to the young woman standing near him. She was his wife. He introduced me to his brother, too, and to many of his men. He had fifty people in his group; two were Jews, and Kalman and I made four.

My recovery took several weeks. They brought me animal fats to rub on my wounds. With Felyuk, things were different than in my own group. Although Felyuk too had no connection with Moscow at that time, he had more experience than

I had. He planned everything himself — he worked out every detail himself, although he, like me, wasn't a professional soldier. He was a shoemaker by occupation. Felyuk's ace-in-hand was that he had his informers in almost every town, village, and hamlet. He knew things I had had absolutely no way of knowing. He knew exactly what was going on almost everywhere at all times. His informers knew how to reach him, and he was in constant contact with them. All this, of course, I found out later.

Shortly after I was accepted into Felyuk's group, our situation heated up. The Germans smelled that it was Felyuk's group — they called us "bandits" — who had killed collaborators and Germans, human beasts who butchered innocent people. They knew that Felyuk's men had flattened and burned important buildings and houses. So they sent key army units after us, and we had to move very rapidly. We couldn't remain long in one place. We could almost feel the pressure in the air.

At this time, Felyuk went away for several days. We didn't know where he went. When he went away, he would leave his adjutant in command; this adjutant came from Felyuk's own home village, Klopochin, which was situated four or five kilometers from Trochenbrot. When Felyuk returned, he was very upset. He called a special meeting of all his men. That was his way of doing things: for serious business, he used to call everybody together and propose a plan. He would ask his own men for their opinions, but Felyuk always had the last word. This was, of course, quite proper; he was, after all, the commander. However, he would always consider his men's opinions and advice carefully.

Felyuk explained that there was a certain murderer in a small hamlet near Trostyanets. As I explained before, whenever the Germans massacred Jews, a small percentage of the doomed Jews would escape into the woods. Mothers with small children would get separated, and children wandered around alone in the woods. Felyuk explained to us that this murderer was going around in the woods looking especially for such small Jewish children. He would stab these children and kill them. That was his greatest pleasure. Besides several hundred Jewish children (he kept score), he had also stabbed twelve Komsomols (members of the Young Communist League). Felyuk said, "Whatever happens, we *must* capture this murderer alive!" This beast lived in a hamlet, and the head of this hamlet collaborated with the Germans, so Felyuk said we would have to capture him too.

Felyuk asked me for my opinion about this operation. I said that we should postpone this mission until the Germans became quieter. Then, we would surely launch the operation. Felyuk stood up, came right over to me, and exclaimed, "This is what *you* say? He stabbed so many of your innocent brothers and sisters — 4-, 5- and 6-year-old children — and you can say such a thing? No, sir, my dear Kohn. We're going to send four or five men on this mission *now*, and you're the first man I'm picking for this job!" He evidently had not planned to send me.

Felyuk gathered four of us together, and we made a plan. Felyuk would come to the hamlet, ostensibly from Kolki, whose jurisdiction this hamlet was under; he would come as a leader of the Ukrainian nationalist police, with whom this murderer collaborated so closely. The excuse for Felyuk's visit would be that, since this murderer worked so well for the Germans, they wanted to honor and promote him. So Felyuk would go into his house, talk to him, and then lead him out of the house to a wagon 180 meters away. The driver was to be Itzik, a Jewish boy. One of our men would be at the window and another at the door. If Felyuk noticed something amiss or the murderer tried to jump out the door or window, we should, if it was unavoidable, kill him. But if we heard the murderer coming out normally, we were to melt away into the darkness and let him get into the wagon. We agreed that, if things went according to plan and he was in the wagon, we would meet 400 meters away at the community leader's house. We would also put the community leader into the wagon, and we would take them both into the forest to put them on trial.

So we went to the hamlet. When Felyuk, disguised as a police official, knocked at the door, a woman answered. Felyuk's first words were "Slava Ukraine!" The Banderovtsy, instead of saying "Heil Hitler," would say "Slava Ukraine." Felyuk asked, in Ukrainian, "Where is your husband?" She answered that he was sleeping; he was very tired. Felyuk said, "You have to wake him up. I've been sent from the Ukrainian SD* in Kolki. Your husband has accomplished great things; he has been very worthy — that's why I've been sent here."

The woman woke her husband up. Again, the "Slava Ukraine" greeting. Felyuk said, "We've all heard of your worthy deeds and great accomplishments. That's why I've been sent — to bring you to headquarters." The murderer said, "You hear, my wife? Put some *varenikes*** and vodka on the table!" Felyuk couldn't hurry things — he had to go along. So they started to drink. They drank for Stefan Bandera, for other nationalist leaders, and for Adolf Hitler. They had downed five or six glasses when this nationalist went over to the corner of the room and picked up a stick, which was a meter and a half in length; a bayonet was attached to the end of the stick. He said, "You see this stick with the bayonet? So many

* Security Police.
** Ukrainian dumplings

dirty Jews I've killed with it, and they sprout up like mush-rooms! Every time I think I've finally cleaned them out, they grow again like mushrooms, those little shits! I've polished off hundreds of Jews and Komsomols!" So Felyuk said, "Ah, that's why they sent me. We know about your accomplishments, how faithful you are to our cause." The murderer asked, "Where are we going?" Felyuk answered, "We're going to the headquarters at Kolki; there you'll probably get the medal and a promotion." The murderer wanted to take his own wagon and horses. "They're terrific horses — I lifted them from a filthy Jew; you've never seen such magnificent horses!" Felyuk answered, "No, my wagon driver is waiting; we must leave right away because there are bandits* hanging around. Who knows what can happen? So let's go!"

As soon as they came out, we melted away. Felyuk sat him down on the wagon and said, "Now I'm going for the community leader. He is to be decorated too. It'll only take me ten or fifteen minutes." So the murderer was sitting there with this Jewish boy, Itzik. Itzik was about 17 years old; he spoke pure, literary Ukrainian. He wore a specially embroidered Ukrainian blouse. We had moved off about a hundred meters and were waiting. Suddenly, we heard two shots from where the horses and wagon were standing. We ran back immediately. We saw that the murderer was lying on the ground a few meters from the wagon. He looked dead. We asked Itzik, "What did you do? You knew we needed him alive!" The boy answered, "As soon as Felyuk left, the murderer said that he wanted to have a drink of water. He wanted to return to his house." Itzik said to him, "Don't go. There are bandits around. When my chief returns, we must leave at once." Several minutes later, the murderer started

* In other words, partisans.

[80]

again with the water, and Itzik gave him the same reply. The nationalist then exclaimed, "What am I — a prisoner?" And he started to smell a rat; he started to suspect that something was wrong. Itzik tried to reassure him. He said, "I have a police order — we must stay here and wait for the other two. Then we must drive to Kolki." After a minute, the murderer leaped off the wagon and took off. It was an extremely dark night. How Itzik managed to hit him I don't know, but the bullet did hit the shoulder. Felyuk, who had come running, decided that we wouldn't go after the community leader at that time. A shot had echoed all over the place there — everybody must have heard it. Felyuk said that we would put the body into the wagon and throw it out somewhere.

We put the body in the wagon, covered it with hay, and several of us sat on it. Then we drove away. After ten kilometers, we heard a groan. The murderer's blood had apparently congealed, and as he regained consciousness, he felt the pain. As soon as he groaned, we stopped the wagon and jumped out. Felyuk grabbed him by the hair. "You lowest of the low — you're still alive?" The murderer started to beg, "I'll work with you, I'll collaborate with you!" While we had been covering the ten kilometers, we had been talking amongst ourselves; we thought that he was dead, so we had talked openly. We went another fifteen kilometers into the woods and took the murderer out of the wagon. He embraced Felyuk's feet and started to blubber and whine. Felyuk gave him a sharp kick in the head, and he said, "Listen, and listen well, you vermin. We are not going to be the ones who will try you. Those who will put you on trial will be the innocent people who you killed. We'll just try you in their name. It's those guiltless, defenseless children _who never had a chance — they will bring justice down on your head!"

For half an hour, Felyuk spoke. The forest echoed. We all

cried. We felt as if we were choking; we couldn't stand it. Felyuk told the murderer why he was being tried and in whose name — in the name of human decency and right-eousness. He expressly mentioned the innocent Jewish chil-dren, and mentioned the Komsomols. He said, "What did you have against 4- and 5-year-old children? What *had* they ever done to you? What *could* they have done to you?" I've seen many trials, and I've heard many brilliant prosecutors and judges. Felyuk wasn't a prosecutor, and he wasn't a judge, but his heart was talking. Someone with a prepared speech couldn't have spoken that way. Only a person who is living through such a heart-rending experience could speak like that. His speech lasted half an hour. Then he said to Itzik, the driver, "You started the job; now finish him off!" They took the murderer aside and executed him. Then, as we moved off to another place, Felyuk said, "I wanted to take them both alive, keep them a short time, and show them to other people as an example and a lesson. Things didn't work out quite as I had planned. I wanted to show others what happens to those who shed innocent blood."

Then, in 1942, when the earth was burning, the fact that there were such Aleksandr Fyodorovich Felyuks should be underlined and remembered. And treasured. This hap-pened at the beginning of 1943 — I don't know the exact date. At that time, I had been with Felyuk's group for several weeks.

A month after this incident, Felyuk gathered us together and explained that there was a small town not far from Kolki, where one German was stationed and seven or eight Uk-rainian nationalist police. They had done terrible things in this town of 3,000 to 4,000 people and in the surrounding area. Felyuk said that we had to clean the German and his associates out of there. We prepared twenty men for this operation. Felyuk would enter the town on market day as a fowl seller. Once a week the peasants from the surrounding area came to the town to trade in cows, chickens, and the like. Kalman Klein went on this mission, as did I. Ten men were to go into the town, and ten were to be stationed around the town to secure the escape route.

Felyuk took a wagon, loaded it with ducks, hens, and geese, and drove into town. He parked the wagon close to the Ukrainian police headquarters. Several hours passed, and Felyuk sold his merchandise. The Ukrainian police sauntered over; they wanted a drink. Felyuk satisfied them and drank with them. After some time, somebody — not a policeman — recognized Felyuk and informed the police. Felyuk was known there because before the war, in 1940 and 1941, he had worked in Tsuman as an area truant officer for the local school authorities (although by trade he was a shoemaker). Just as Felyuk had turned our wagon around and was preparing to leave, a policeman came over and asked for his papers. Felyuk needed (and had) a special permit, as a peasant-farmer, to travel and sell his fowl. The policeman examined Felyuk's papers, looked them over up and down, and said, "You'll have to come with me into the headquarters building." But we had mined the police headquarters and were ready to blow it sky high. Felyuk went to the police building and entered with the policeman. Our ten men, who were in the town in various disguises, filtered through to the police headquarters building and surrounded it. In the main corridor, Felyuk, with his bare hands, strangled the policeman. He then bolted from the corridor, leaped out of the building, slammed the door shut, and moved off a short way. It all took only a few seconds. Then our men blew the building up. The peasants and townspeople saw and heard the explosion, and a big panic ensued. Not all the policemen were inside that building when we blew it up. The others tried to flee the town. We had our men on the outskirts of the town, so we grabbed the rest of the policemen — five of them — and we finished them off.

Trochenbrot had had about 500 Jewish families, and Ignatovka about 120 Jewish families. The two towns were now empty — everybody had been slaughtered. The whole area of the two towns had a ghostly appearance. Only the grass was growing. The Germans used enormous machines to bundle this hay and collect it for shipment to the front. There were hundreds of tons of bundled hay already prepared for shipment, with seven or eight policemen left to guard it. And there were about a hundred trucks parked on the road, waiting to transport it. Felyuk gathered us together. He had had many Jewish friends in those two villages — he used to mention them by name. He told us, "Look, guys! Tomorrow the Germans are supposed to ship this hay out on the trucks. Jews are useless to those German bastards — they killed them off to the last man, woman, and child — but Jewish hay is very good. Tomorrow they are going to transport the hay to fuel their war machine. The trucks are already parked in readiness ten or twelve kilometers from Trochenbrot. Let the whole damn thing burn — trucks and hay together."

Felyuk sent two groups. One group was to "take care" of the trucks, and the other group was responsible for the "safety" of the hay. Not a single blade of hay was left; not a single one of those trucks would ever be usable again. In my official partisan record, Felyuk entered this incident of the hay-burning.

The Germans were vigorous in their hunt for Felyuk, so we had to move constantly. Felyuk's wife was with us, as was his brother — a younger brother — and several cousins.

Felyuk had a year-old daughter, whom he couldn't take into the woods, so he left this infant with his grandfather (the child's great-grandfather). I saw this old man. He was then over 90 years old. He was also called Aleksandr Fyodorovich. Once every month or so, Felyuk would sneak into the village with his wife to look in on the baby. On these visits, we used to come at midnight, stay all night, and pull out at 5 in the morning.

Among our people, in Felyuk's group, there was a German agent, an infiltrator. He notified the Germans that we would come to that town on a certain date. But we were lucky. We came a day earlier. I asked Felyuk, after the war, whether he had purposely changed the date or whether our arrival a day earlier was a pure accident. He replied, "Kohn, many times I would give a date and then go into action a day earlier or later, but in this particular case it was more accident than calculation." So we came to the town a day earlier. The next day the Germans surrounded the whole village and sealed it tightly — very tightly. They chased everybody out of their houses. There were also German sympathizers in Klopochin, but I must say that, oddly enough, 99 percent of the villagers of Klopochin were decent people with warm hearts.

After chasing everybody out of their homes, the Germans selected 127 men. Those men presumably sympathized with the Russians or had shown sympathy towards Jews. The Germans put these men aside and sent the rest home. Felyuk's grandfather was among the 127 men who had been selected; a German officer saw that he was a very old man, with a long, long beard, so he told him to go home. However, they did not release the baby. The old man, on arriving home, sat down on his front stoop. He was without his great-grandaughter; he saw that this neighbor was not here, another had been taken away, and still another was gone, so he said, "Ah, they took my great-grandaughter, let them take me too!" And he returned to the 127 men.

When he rejoined the men and took the child back into his arms, a terrible thing happened. The leader of the Ukrainian police of that area — his family name was Sisco — recognized the baby. Sisco had been a teacher and had worked with Felyuk when Felyuk served as a truant officer. Sisco told the Germans, "This is the bandit's child. Let me take care of this matter." Under Sisco's direction they dug a hole, put the baby in, and buried her alive. The 127 men were led into a hollow and all 127 of them were machine-gunned to death.

On hearing what had happened, Felyuk kept control of himself. His wife, Vera, was unconsolable. For a week, she was in terrible condition. I never saw Felyuk cry, but I saw that he went sleepless night after night. At that time, we went on more revenge missions than at any other time. A night didn't pass without a major operation being carried out. Felyuk really took revenge for his baby. We used to move thirty or forty kilometers every night on these missions, and these revenge operations continued for many months.

Once, Felyuk sent ten men on a mission, and they returned with a poster in Ukrainian. It was a small poster, produced on a typewriter. It said, "Whoever captures the watchmaker and kills him will get two kilograms of salt; whoever brings him in alive will get five kilograms of salt." I must admit that this poster sent me into a depression. I thought, "God, two kilos of salt for a human being — is that all that a life is worth?" I became very morose; I even stopped talking for a while. One day, Felyuk noticed I was depressed, but he was unaware that the men had given me the poster. He asked, "What's wrong, Kohn?" I handed him the poster and told him to read it. So he read it and started to laugh heartily. He said, "Ah, Kohn, you should be proud!" I asked, "Why?"

[86]

Felyuk said, "Look, they're offering five kilos for you. The rate for ordinary people is half a kilo, so this shows that they think that you're that much more valuable. Kohn, if they think you're so much more dangerous to them, then you *should* be more dangerous. You should kill even more of them, you should take even more revenge!" He slapped me playfully on the back and said, "C'mon, Kohn, let's go! There's work to be done!" With those words, I snapped out of my depression. Ah, Felyuk was a great leader! With a few words he brought me out of the darkness.

A terrible German agent was operating in our region. He himself didn't kill, nor did he overtly condemn anybody with his words. But terrible things happened as a result of his collaboration with the Germans. At this time, Felyuk was so feverishly active that he fell on this collaborator's trail. "Whatever happens," he told us, "we mustn't bug it up as we did before — we *must* capture this agent alive! If we take him alive, then I'll find out who gave us away when I came to my village to see the baby."

We were six or seven men on this operation. We thought we had made sure that the collaborator would be at home. However, when we came that night, he wasn't there. We surrounded the place and searched every square inch of it, but he just wasn't there. For us to leave the place and plan to return some other time made no sense at all, because he would never return there again. Our men were sure that he must be at home. They had seen him go into his house that evening.

A typical house in a hamlet at that time was built around a central corridor. One door led to an area where the cows were kept; other doors led to the sleeping room, a kitchen, and a pantry. There was also a closet for clothing. We searched *everywhere*. We went through the clothes in the

[87]

closet carefully. We couldn't find that bandit. The only course of action left to us was to set the house on fire. At that point I had an idea. Hay was stored in the attic. I said I would go up there and look around.

I climbed into the attic. The place was covered with hay. Some light filtered through from the outside, so I was able to see. Hay was piled high all over the attic. Assuming that the bandit *must* be hiding in the hay, I took a stick and systematically started poking it through the hay, covering every square meter. I was bent over, leaning forward at an angle as I moved along, pushing my stick into the hay. By the time I had made ten sweeps one way and ten sweeps the other way, I must have been getting close to his hiding place. I was making one of my sweeps away from him, with my back to his hiding place, when he made his move. There was a small door leading to the yard. He figured that, while I was moving away from him and facing in the opposite direction, he would shoot me and jump out through that door. So he fired twice, and one shot hit me. I was lucky — there was a metal pan hanging between me and him, so the bullet was slowed down by its passage through the pan. But I was nevertheless severely wounded.

When I fell, the bandit covered me with hay. He was in the process of jumping out of the window when my associates grabbed him. Blood was pouring from me as if a tap had been turned on. Felyuk's men had to search for me in all that hay. When they found me, I had lost consciousness. They took me down and bandaged my wound with a towel. A short time later I regained consciousness. When they put me in the wagon, I saw them putting the bandit in the wagon too.

We took the bandit into the woods where we were at home. We held him several days and found out about all his activites. So he was put on trial, just as the murderer of Jewish children had been tried before, and he was condemned to death. Felyuk said that he wanted very, very much that I should finish that bandit off, but he saw that I didn't have the strength. I was too weak. So he said, "At the very least, let him be finished off before your eyes!" And they ended that bandit's career then. Felyuk wrote a detailed letter to the Ukrainian and German police in which he explained exactly why the agent had been executed.

There was no medical doctor in Felyuk's group; there wasn't even a *feldsher* (medic). For several weeks Felyuk's men trundled me around in a wagon. I was weakening steadily, and the wound was filling with pus. Once, when Felyuk came to me and asked, "How do you feel, Naum?"* I answered, "I feel very bad, Aleksandr Fyodovich. I'm sinking away. I have one favor to ask of you. I'm not going to live much longer — I know that. And I know that you can't save me. So you'll trundle me with wagons for another week, another two weeks — but we know what the end will be, and, meanwhile, it's trouble for you and torture for me. Find me some poison, and let me drink it, and that'll be it. I would want that you yourself finish me off, but I know that you won't be able to bring yourself to do it. Felyuk, you know who I am; you know all about my family. Take an interest. Maybe some of my brothers and sisters will remain alive. Tell them that there was such and such a Naum in your group. You know where I'm from." I was very close to Felyuk. We were very open with each other, and he did indeed know all about my family.

Felyuk looked at me sharply and said, "So! So that's it, eh? Listen, Naum — you haven't done very much so far! You have a lot of Germans to kill yet! You've done the equivalent

* In Yiddish and in English my name is Nahum; in Ukrainian, it is Naum.

of a drop in the ocean. If you'll go away, and another will go away, and another . . . who will be left to take care of the Germans?"

I replied, "Felyuk, don't carry on so. I know that I'm finished and nobody and nothing can help me." I then called Vera, his wife, over to me. I said, "Vera, talk your husband into finishing me off. I see that my condition is deteriorating. I'm suffering, and I'm a burden to you." Partisans had to move rapidly, and carrying an extremely sick person on a wagon through the forest was a cumbersome burden. Vera started to cry, and said, "Naum, stop talking that way!" A few days later I badgered her again and received a similar response.

Some days later, Felyuk came to me and said, "Naum, I'm taking you to a doctor." I said, "What? How? With Germans all around?" But he insisted, "*I am taking you to a doctor*. You have a big debt to repay to the 'dear' Germans, and so far you've repaid only a small part of it." Felyuk and three men put me on a wagon and took me to a hamlet, Yarmelko, twenty or twenty-five kilometers from Lutsk. He carried me into a peasant's house, put the makeshift stretcher down, and called the peasant over. Felyuk told him, "Listen here! I'm leaving our man with you. Nobody must know about him — not your neighbor, nor your friends." (His closest neighbor, Vitkovsky, lived 200 meters from his house). "If you're planning a little 'trick,' or a 'surprise' — well, you and your wife and your five children will all pay for it. And the price will be very, very high! I know that it's not going to be easy for you to keep a sick man here. Don't worry about food — I'm going to leave you enough food to feed your family for a year. You'll have enough salt for ten families." Felyuk didn't mention that I was a Jew — if I was a partisan, that was more than enough!

The peasant, Ostrovsky, hesitated, but what choice did he have? He was facing the business end of a gun. They left him a killed pig, a sack of flour, and other things. They showed his wife how to clean the wound until they returned.

I lay in Ostrovsky's house for one day, two days, a week. I even started to think that I had been dumped there permanently. Maybe I had been abandoned. But I couldn't believe that *that* man — my Felyuk — could do such a thing. He had left a revolver with me and had told me, "Naum, if, God forbid, something should happen, you should shoot, you should fight as long as you can. But remember — your last bullet is for you yourself. Above all, you must never fall into their hands alive."

One night, after ten or twelve days, at 1 or 2 A.M., we heard tapping on the windows of Ostrovsky's house. Felyuk and his men were there, and they led a man with blindfolded eyes into the house. They unbound the blindfold. This man whom they brought was a doctor. He had been ordered by Felyuk's men to bring his medical equipment with him. They had kidnapped him from a hospital or clinic about fifty kilometers away, where he had been working for the Germans. Since he had been brought to a different area, he had no idea where he was. He must have been a surgeon, although they called him *panye feldsher* — which is what they called all male medical personal. He extracted the bullet, which was still in me, surrounded by much pus. For security reasons, Felyuk's men didn't let him exchange one word with the Ostrovsky family.

I want to underline to you what kind of deed it was to bring this doctor like that to me. The doctor spent two or three days in the house with me; he had to follow up the case after he had dug out the bullet. Finally, he said that the healing process had begun — I would recover. He left bandages. He taught Mrs. Ostrovsky how to bandage the wound and clean it properly. He said that in a month or six weeks I would be fully recovered. And I started slowly to feel better; every day brought me back more strength, but a problem developed. I felt that I could walk; I could get around on makeshift crutches. However, I had been hit in such a place (just below the rectum) that any movement ripped the wound open. I was young — 23 years old — and that was in my favor, but every time I tried to walk the wound opened up. So Felyuk's men returned to the doctor and told him about the open wound. He said that I had to stay in bed, absolutely still , for three months. I was not supposed to walk at all. Although that doctor didn't know who he was treating and where he had been, my comrades made him swear solemnly that he would tell no one about his "adventure." If he talked about what he had seen, then he could say goodbye to his family and to everything.

Felyuk came to me about a month later. He brought enough food for Ostrovsky's family, and of course he left the finest food for me. On such visits, he used to spend half a day with me, or a day at most. Two or three comrades used to drop in on me, always at night. By this time, I had been in Ostrovsky's house for four months, and I had started to walk a little. Felyuk told me that the Soviet partisan command had dropped some men in his area, and Felyuk had coordinated his activities to aid this jump. Three groups had been dropped earlier, but all of the members of these groups had been killed. These latest parachutists would also have been killed, but they met Felyuk the day after they jumped. One was a radio operator, Nina Alexeyevna; another was called Alexeyev; and a third man completed the trio. Following the orders of the partisan high command, one of the jumpers became the leader of Felyuk's group, and Felyuk was to serve

[92]

as his adjutant. But in reality it was Felyuk who ran things, because the man who had been parachuted was quite green; he didn't know very much.

I begged Felyuk, on one of his visits to take me back with him. But he replied, "No, wait till my next visit. You're close to complete recovery, you're almost ready." And he explained to me where our partisan group was encamped, about eighteen kilometers from Ostrovsky's house. I knew exactly where they were after Felyuk explained their position to me. I hardly knew the towns, but I knew the forests backwards and forwards, because those forests had become my home. Before the war, I could never have imagined how a person could get to know forests in such a detailed and exact way.

I wanted urgently to return with Felyuk because of a change that was taking place — the Ukrainians and the Poles had started to fight. At first, the Ukrainians had helped the Germans, so the Germans kept them as "favorites" for a year or a year and a half. While the Ukrainians were with the Germans, they had hit the Poles. Then the Ukrainians saw that the Germans were exploiting them, so they started to take to the woods and form assassin bands, nationalist terrorist bands. These were not decent, partisan groups; these Ukrainian nationalist bands were out to make the area clean of Jews, clean of everybody except themselves. So the Germans took the Poles, made them into police, and turned them on the Ukrainians. In this way, Poles and Ukrainians would kill each other and forget about the Germans. In Yarmelko, where Ostrovsky's house was located, the houses almost alternated — one was Ukrainian, the next Polish, the next Ukrainian, and so on. They had been living as peaceful neighbors for over a century, and suddenly they started to burn each other's houses down. That was why I begged

Felyuk to take me with him. But he insisted that I was still weak and that in two weeks he would come for me and I would rejoin the group.

By a week after Felyuk left, the Ukrainian-Polish antagonism had come very close to the clearing where Ostrovsky's house was located. The peasants started to kill each other; Ukrainians and Poles were burning down each other's places. I was no longer using crutches — I used a big stick. There was a small forest very close to Ostrovsky's house — maybe hundred meters away — and I used to spend much time there, waiting for Felyuk. I was better off in the forest than in the house, which might come under attack at any moment during this Ukrainian-Polish feuding.

Ostrovsky was very frightened; he could not continue to live in his house. He told me that he was leaving to go live with his brother, and he suggested that I come with him — he would take me in a wagon. I refused because I felt that, if Felyuk no longer knew where I was, I would lose my trump card. Besides, I wanted to get back into action. I was feeling better. In any case, I wasn't 100 percent confident of Ostrovsky.

So, when I saw that the house-burning was getting closer, I went off on my own. I knew more or less where Felyuk was, but it took me three full days to cover the eighteen kilometers. I moved very slowly; every two or three kilometers I had to lie down. I had my revolver. I finally came to the village near Felyuk's position. He had told me that a trail went from that village into the woods, and that he was in the forest, at the end of that trial. I looked for the trail, and I sought the forest that was supposed to be nearby, but I didn't see it at all. I couldn't ask anybody. I was weak. The police were swarming all over the place, and I had no papers, no pass — nothing. Only my revolver.

[94]

Just at dawn the next day, I went to a house near the edge of the village to get some food. You could get food then only with a "convincer," a gun. A revolver was gold, diamonds, *everything* — without it you were regarded as a cockroach. With it you became a respected person. Even with my revolver, I was so weak, they could easily have tried to jump me. But I got the food, and as I went out with it, I noticed a cart filled with hay. I lay down in the hay and started eating. A peasant came over to a nearby cart and began filling it with hay. While he was working, I moved in on him. Don't forget, I had a long beard, I was haggard, and I carried the revolver in an obviously menacing way. I looked a sight!

Weak as I was, I was at the peasant's side in an instant. I said to him, "Listen to me! I'm a Jew. Show me where the partisans are!" He said, "I don't mix into such matters. I don't want to get involved." There were people like that then. I told him, "I know you don't want to get involved, but now you *are* involved! If you don't help me, you know what's in store for you! You must take me to the partisans!" It was dawn; there was dew on the ground, and you could see the impression of footprints. The farmer said, "Look, several hours ago the partisans must have taken hay from here, and if you'll follow this trail you'll come to them. You'll definitely find them." However, I didn't trust him. Ninety percent of these peasants told lies. He could have been preparing to call the Germans the moment I left. So I told him, "*Nothing* is going to help you. You're going to have to lead me along the trail yourself, and you'll have to do it slowly — I can't move fast. You'll move two or three meters in front of me. If you make one false move or try to take off — the first bullet will be for you. So decide on your course of action now." He saw that he had no choice in the whole matter, so he said, "What about my cart?" I said, "Leave it here with the horse. Nobody

[95]

is going to steal it. During the day nobody will come; partisans only come at night. And if the partisans do take it, I guarantee that you'll get it back."

And so we moved off, following the trail, which led us back through the village and out the other side. I was very uneasy because people were beginning to come out. I looked a sight, and in such villages everybody knew everybody else — a stranger would be spotted immediately, but I had no other way. The peasant led me along the trail until we were six or seven kilometers beyond the village. Then he said, "You see, the trail is continuing — it's so easy to follow it. You don't really need my help." I said, "Keep going, keep going — nothing will help you." So he went another three kilometers. Then he lay down on the grass and said, "I'm exhausted. I've lived enough." It was true — he was elderly. "If you want to, shoot me! I can't go on any more. I swear to you by all that is holy that this is the trail to the partisans." I said, "Okay, but show me your passport. If you are telling a lie, and I get away, you'll pay for it with your life." He answered, "I'm telling the truth, but in a village we have no passports." That was true. "I have a baptism certificate at home, but it's not with me now. It's up to you. You can see the blades of hay on the ground that we've been following.* Follow them and you'll come to the partisans. If you don't believe me, shoot me!" I made him tell me his family name and the location of his house in the village. He knew, and I knew, that finding him would be no problem. And then I let him go.

I followed the hay trail for another three or four kilometers. The trail led me to a road, where cars and trucks were moving. I had to walk along that road — I had no choice. I thought that perhaps he had purposely fed me false information, to push me into the Germans' claws, but I had no

* Pieces of hay fall off a moving, hay-filled cart.

choice — I had to continue. I had been away from the house for five or six days, and I was at the end of my rope. I saw that the road joined a highway and continued along it for 200 or 300 meters. Germans were driving by, but they were moving rapidly. They were afraid to stop. Then the trail left the road and plunged into a nearby forest. I started to feel a bit optimistic. I proceeded for about another kilometer when I heard, from all around, "Halt! Stand still! Hands up! Hands on high!"

I was hoping it was Felyuk's men, but I was afraid to turn around — maybe they were Banderovtsy, who were also in the woods by this time. But, as I turned ever so slowly, I saw a white armband with a red Russian star. Felyuk's men didn't wear such insignia, but believe me, I breathed a sigh of relief. I stood still but I didn't raise my hands. Again they barked, "Hands up!" I understood Ukrainian, but it was still hard for me to speak it — I used to mix it with Polish. Three or four men approached me very cautiously, and I didn't recognize one face among them. They weren't my guys. I stood still, with my makeshift cane. They asked where I was going? I said, "I'm going to you." They asked, "Who is 'you'?" I said, "The partisans." They said if I were armed, and when I told them of my revolver, they said, "Hand it over!" I answered, "You know you don't ask a partisan to surrender his arm." One of them nodded and said, "Okay, put it down in front of you and sit down." Put it down or not put it down — I saw that it was no longer a life-and-death question, because I was among partisans. But where I was and who they were exactly, I still did not know. I heard their Russian conversation, and I could recognize certain words. One of them told me to remain seated, and, leaving a Ukrainian near me, the rest left.

I had been sitting like that for an hour, when two partisans came riding in on horses, followed by a few others. They were wearing hats with Soviet insignia. One of the horsemen was a Spaniard, and he spoke very broken Russian — the same kind I spoke. But he was the commander of the group guarding the whole partisan encampment nearby. The other partisan on horseback was an older man, Franz Ignatovich. I remember him well because after I was with the group for a year Franz and I became quite close. He was born in Poland, and he was a communist; he came to the Soviet Union in 1918. I came from Sieradz, and he came from Czenstochov, about eighty kilometers away, so we used to talk together often. His wife is still alive; she was also a partisan. But Franz was killed by Banderovtsy three or four months after the war. He was a very fine man and served as the head of a collective farm.

The two partisans asked me where I was from and with whom I had served. I told them that I had been in a partisan group commanded by Aleksandr Fyodorovich Felyuk, that I had been injured in a certain engagement with the enemy, and so on. And I told them, "Felyuk must be around here, and I've been looking for him." They didn't answer me directly, and from their small talk among themselves I could learn nothing. They questioned me for about twenty minutes and then left. A third man came over and said, "Get up and follow us!" I followed them for several kilometers, but they were going too fast on their horses, so I shouted to them to slow down. I was still quite weak, and I had to lean heavily on the thick cane. They were very considerate and slowed down.

When I was first challenged by the partisans, I hadn't stumbled on their encampment. I had fallen into a forward position ten kilometers from their encampment, which was surrounded by such positions. Every half a kilometer around the circumference of the encampment there were two men manning an outer warning post. Aleksandr Fyodorovich had not had that degree of organization, which was more formally military.

The horseback riders led me deep, very deep into the forest, and we finally approached the main encampment. I saw a whole city there! I couldn't believe my eyes! My own group had numbered eighteen men; Felyuk had fifty men, and I thought that his group was the most modern and organized possible. But here I saw hundreds if not thousands of men! I saw cars, trucks, cavalry, a hospital; I saw antitank guns, artillery pieces, horses, cows . . . it was a whole new world for me. I couldn't imagine that these were partisans. They looked like a regular army. As I was being led in, I saw that they were slaughtering cows for their kitchens. I was quite bewildered. They took me to the center of the encampment, to the headquarters of the command company. Here the whole business of interrogation started again.

Another man came in from the headquarters staff and questioned me, at first for only an hour or so, since he saw that I was weak. Later, they interrogated me for a full day, and they asked about everything. They covered practically every day of my existence, and then they took me to the field hospital. Imagine — in the forest a hospital with eight or nine doctors! The chief doctor was a Jew named Albert Venyaminovich Tsessarsky. He had been taken from his fourth course at the university and dropped there by parachute. They had many nurses in the hospital, too. The doctors checked me over very carefully, especially where I had been injured. They took care of my wound. They laughed at my beard and cut it off. They really hadn't believed that I was 23 years old while I had that long beard. They gave me a much-needed haircut too. I was treated for two days, and then I underwent another full day of interrogation. However, the whole atmosphere had now changed — the inter-

[99]

rogator were smiling, cracking jokes, and their whole attitude to me had changed. What happened was that as soon
as I made contact with them, they had radioed Moscow about
me. The partisan high command in Moscow knew where
Felyuk was, and they were in constant contact with him. They
obtained my record from Felyuk and all the information
about my past, and the high command forwarded this record
and information to the interrogators. If one thing I told
them hadn't coincided with the facts . . .! So on this last day
of questioning they were friendly, and they even fed me a
name or a place from my own past when I became tired. I
was with friends now, not interrogators. Let me tell you — it
felt great!

I still had no idea where Felyuk was (I found out much
later that he was only five kilometers away!). I told my interrogators that I wanted to rejoin his group. I told them that I
had been left in Ostrovsky's house with the understanding
that, when I was well, I would rejoin the group. The interrogators told me, "No, rejoining Felyuk is not possible for
you. You must be completely and professionally healed; we
have surgeons here. Felyuk probably doesn't even have an
ordinary doctor." I thought it over and saw that they were
right. My own recent experience had been proof enough of
that.

I was then taken to a group called *podryvnaya gruppa* —
these were mine-layers and dynamiters; in other words, a
demolition squad. I was now to begin a new chapter in my
life, as a member of Medvedev's atrád, one of the most
famous regiments in the Soviet partisan organization.

PART THREE

CARL A. RUDISILL LIBRARY
LENOIR RHYNE COLLEGE

There were many partisan atráds operating in German-occupied territory. In the Rovno area of the Ukraine (Rovno Oblast) alone there were 30,000 partisans, who were organized in twenty-five or more atráds. But Medvedev's atrád was special — it had an exceptional status. It specialized in espionage, information gathering. The general staff of all of the other partisan atráds was in Kiev, under the command of Voroshilov, but Medvedev's atrád was directed by the Moscow general staff, which also controlled only one other partisan atrád. No other body had any direct authority over Medvedev's atrád.

Consisting of 1,500 partisans, this atrád had been created largely for a single purpose: to support the work of one man, first known to the Germans as Lieutenant Paul Siebert, and later as Hauptmann (Captain) Paul Siebert; to a few members of our atrád he was known as Grachov. After the war, I found out, from Medvedev's books, that his real name was Kuznetsov. In Medvedev's atrád no more than thirty men had any knowledge of him. Supporting Kuznetsov caused our atrád's involvement in many battles, because the Germans knew about our work — they felt our atrád's presence. No senior German officer, however high his rank, could sleep untroubled at night, all because of Kuznetsov and Medvedev's atrád. After the war, over ten books were written about Medvedev's atrád and its singular achievements. To join our atrád was very difficult because our command staff was extremely selective.

At the beginning of 1942, a group of twenty men was parachuted from Moscow into the Sarny area, not far from Rovno. That area is called Tolstoles. Another group, numbering eighteen people, was soon parachuted there, and it was followed by a third group and a fourth. One of these groups was blown off course by strong winds, and all of its members landed in German hands; they were all shot. The remaining three groups united and started to organize themselves for the long fight that lay ahead. They numbered seventy partisans, with Medvedev as their leader. At the beginning, Medvedev's chief of operations was Maria Fortus. After a short time, she was replaced by Aleksandr Aleksandrovich Lukin. These seventy partisans were fortunate because there were already many small groups operating in those forests, like Felyuk's band and my eighteen-man group. These small groups had crystallized independently as an opposition to the Germans and the Banderovtsy. They provided an operational base for the trained personnel dropped by Moscow. One of these independent groups — an important one — was led by Kolya (Nikolay) Strutinsky.

Strutinsky came from a small village, Bude, forty kilometers from Rovno. His family was a very poor one; his father was of Polish origin, and his mother was Ukrainian. There were nine children in the family. The youngest was 4 or 5 years old. Kolya, at 20 or 21, was the oldest. George Strutinsky, his brother, was a bit younger, and Rostik, another brother, was about 15 or 16 years old. All of Kolya's immediate family — mother, father, brothers, and sisters — were in his forty-five-member group. Other members of Kolya's group came from small hamlets near Bude.

Just as Felyuk was the first in Volhynia, Lutsk Oblast, to organize a partisan group, Kolya Strutinsky was the first to organize a partisan group in the Rovno area. There were no official Soviet partisans yet. As soon as the Germans moved in, Kolya took his family and twenty or thirty men and went into the woods. They formed a tough group, which fought both the German and Banderovtsy murderers. They were soon joined by Kolya Banderchuk and his friends.

Kolya Banderchuk was born in Mezrich, a Jewish *shtetl* about forty kilometers from Rovno. He was a bus driver on the Rovno-Mezrich run before the war. Banderchuk had been in the Polish Army, and he had a rifle. When the Germans came, he took his rifle and went into the woods. Kolya Strutinsky heard about him, so he went to Mezrich to see Banderchuk's mother. She recognized him because he had been her son's friend in prewar days, so she confided in him that her son was hiding in the woods with several friends and would drop in on her from time to time. She told Strutinsky that she would tell her son about his visit.

Kolya Banderchuk had taken to the woods because he saw what the Germans and Banderovtsy were up to, and he didn't want to become their accomplice. He was a Ukrainian — the Banderovtsy would have accepted him with open arms — but he was a warm and sincere human being, a man with a soul and a conscience. His mother told him of Strutinsky's visit, and the two partisans met. Banderchuk decided to join Strutinsky's group and bring his men with him.

When the Banderovtsy heard that Kolya Banderchuk had joined the partisans, they went to his mother, who was then about 45 years old, and said, "You have three days. If your Kolya joins us, we won't bother you. If he doesn't join us within the next three days, we'll be back, and then you'll see something!" These murderers kept their word. They returned in three days because Kolya hadn't joined them. They took his mother, bound her hands and feet, put her in the house, and set the whole place on fire. She was burned to death.

For about a year Strutinsky's group operated like Felyuk's.

Here they killed some particularly vicious police, there they burned some targets of military importance, and so on. By accident, Kolya's men came upon several members of Medvedev's official partisan group in the woods. Medvedev's group was a small one then, a nucleus. Medvedev and Strutinsky held talks, and Strutinsky decided to bring his group into Medvedev's. He saw that strength lay in numbers, and his own group was too small. Kolya Strutinsky could have sat at home — nobody would have bothered him. He was, however, a man of decency and high principles. He saw the need for unity against the butchers and murderers.

Special instructions were radioed to Medvedev's atrád: Moscow was going to parachute a German into the atrád. He was to infiltrate the German military and obtain important strategic information. However, for some reason, that German was never dropped. Kuznetsov was sent instead. Kuznetsov was originally supposed to have served as an aerial reconnaissance spy, but the plans were changed, and he was parachuted into Medvedev's atrád. I learned about this change of plans many years after the war, from an article in a military monthly journal that I read in 1966 or 1967. Kuznetsov was dropped with eight other partisans, including Kolya Gnedyuk, Kolya Prikhodko, Volgov Seredenko, and Grisha Volkov, who later became a company commander.

I cannot overestimate the important of Kuznetsov in our atrád's work and in our final victory. Our whole atrád had been set up to support him in his important work. Even today, new and amazing accomplishments of Kuznetsov come to light.

Nikolay Ivanovich Kuznetsov was born on July 27, 1911, in a village named Zyryanka (Sverdlovsk Oblast) in the Ural Mountains. After primary schooling in the village, Kuznetsov went to the engineering school in Talitsa, a fair-sized town.

He later studied in Sverdlovsk, at the Institute for Foreign Languages, where he specialized in German. Indeed, he was the only student who sat his engineering exams, and took his engineering degree, in German, not Russian. The Soviet Union lacked technical experts at that time, so they imported such personnel from Germany, and these experts were based in Sverdlovsk.

In the early 1930's, an enormous factory, the Uralmasch Works, was built in the Urals. It took four or five years to complete and employed at least 30,000 workers. It was built by special experts sent from Germany. Kuznetsov was always with these German engineers and technicians, and he learned much from them.

Kuznetsov operated as a spy in Rovno for over two years. Every second of his existence there was full of danger, and yet he managed to carry it off successfully. Disguised as a German officer, he ate in their restaurants and attended their social functions. He became the scourge of the mighty "supermen," although he was operating all the while under their very noses.

My personal opinion is that at the beginning of the war a certain Paul Siebert had been captured by the Soviets. Soviet intelligence got to know him very, very well. Every event in his life, however trivial, was carefully studied. Kuznetsov was taught all of this background material until he knew more of Siebert's background than the real Siebert knew. This called for great talent.

Leonid Brezhnev himself recognized the achievements of Kuznetsov in a speech he made on May 9, 1965, the twentieth anniversary of our victory over the Germans. Brezhnev said that our greatest spies and infiltrators in World War II were the famous Richard Sorge and Kuznetsov. Kuznetsov deserved that accolade. Over ten books were written after the war about this extraordinary man, as well as two movies and two plays, which were eagerly received and applauded. Four major monuments were erected in his memory, and visitors from the Soviet Union and even other countries make special tours to the scenes of Kuznetsov's greatest deeds.

In Rovno alone, Kuznetsov killed nine senior generals, and many more colonels and lower-ranking officers. He threw a grenade under the feet of the President of the Reichskommissariat for Political Affairs, General Paul Dargel. By some miracle, Dargel survived, but he lost his feet and was a cripple for the rest of his days. He was sent back to Berlin. Kuznetsov killed the nefarious SS Sturmbannführer Willi Kann, in Rovno. He also killed the general commander of all of the Ukraine. The Nazi brand of perverted "justice" was directed by one ruthless viper, General Alfred Funk, who was chief judge of the Ukraine. This monster was killed by Kuznetsov at the beginning of November, 1943. On the eve of the famous Teheran Conference in 1943, when Stalin, Churchill, and Roosevelt were about to meet, the Germans parachuted a special elite commando assassination squad into the Teheran area. Kuznetsov briefed the Soviet authorities about the operation and the planned assassinations. All of the Germans in the squad were killed before they could do anything.

I shall have much to say later about Kuznetsov, since I was privileged to become one of his many helpers some months after I joined Medvedev's atrád. However, when I first became a member of the atrád at the beginning of 1943, I was attached to the demolition squad, which was responsible for all of the demolition of railroad lines and communication facilities carried out by the atrád. The group had to blow up strategically important railroad targets. I was sent to them because I was a watchmaker and understood timing mechanisms and detonators. The group commander was a tall, handsome man named Malik, who had been a fourth course student in Moscow when the war started. He had been parachuted with one of the original groups that had formed the nucleus of Medvedev's atrád. When I first joined the group, Malik came over to me. I could see from his face that he wasn't a gross man — he had a certain refined look. He spoke to me for about thirty minutes and told me about the functions assigned to his group. He explained what would be expected of me. This group had its own field kitchen, like all of the other groups, and seemed to be a very busy one. I was itching to see action again.

After two days, the group moved out of the encampment to blow up a train. Some men were always left behind, and I was not taken along this time. On certain occasions, only half the group were sent out, but I didn't know this, and I wondered why I had been left behind. When the next mission came and they still didn't take me with them, I went to the commander and said, in very broken language (I wasn't fluent yet), "I didn't come here to eat — I came to accomplish something, to fight Germans!" Malik looked at me and answered, "I understand, Kohn. You'll go, don't worry. Just rest up in the meantime." My inactivity lasted for ten days.

Finally, they selected twenty-five men, and this time I was included. We were told to go to sleep very early. When we slept, we would always post a guard. One man would stay awake and guard, and every two hours the guard would change. The man on guard duty would wake up his replacement, and this guard would, in turn, wake up his replacement two hours later. After we slept, I was given a rifle, and our twenty-five man detachment was led out of the encampment. None of us knew the nature of our mission — where we were going or what we would do there. (This secrecy, as I observed later, was standard partisan security procedure.) It was a warm night. During our preparations, I noticed, with some curiosity, that we had prepared food for the trip. Later I understood that we took food so we wouldn't have to stop anywhere on the way to the target. We wanted to remain unseen. We went thirty to thirty-five kilometers until we came to a small forest. The sun was coming up. We sat all day in that forest so as not to be seen by anybody. We camouflaged ourselves there until evening came, and then we moved closer to our objective — a stretch of railroad track that had to be mined.

Only then did the commander tell us what our job was there: a certain train would go by at a specified time, and it had to be blown up. Half of our men went over to the other side of the tracks, and half remained on the near side. One train passed, a second went by, and then a third. We let them all pass. Then the mines were placed under the tracks. (Sometimes one mine was used; sometimes two were necessary.) They took me and showed how they dug under the tracks and buried the mine. They explained the whole process to me. Sometimes the whole train would be derailed, sometimes only two wagons, and at times only one wagon. Later I saw that most of the time it was the last wagons that would be derailed. In most cases, the beginning of the train would stay on the tracks, and the last cars would derail.

At the designated time, the target train came into view and passed over our mine. An explosion followed. One or two wagons went off the tracks, and the train came to an abrupt stop. A terrific panic ensued. The Germans started to run out of the wagons, and from both sides we shot at them. They didn't know what was happening — it all took place extremely rapidly, in seconds. Our bullets were flying fast and thick. This whole scene had been well prepared. I don't know exactly how many people they lost, but those who ran out of the train were killed. We had arranged a meeting point with the other half of our group, so we crossed over to the other side of the tracks and joined them there. We moved off to a point about fifteen kilometers away, and then began to work our way back to our encampment.

As a member of the demolition squad, I blew up many trains, but I was just following orders; I didn't know why we waited for a specific train at a certain time. Only after the war did I understand how such operations were planned. There were two people from our atrád who worked in Zdolbunov, near Rovno. Zdolbunov was a big train junction from which trains left to various other centers. Our people in Zdolbunov gave us precise information: which trains were going to the front, which carried ammunition, and so on. Our atrád's chief operative in the Zdolbunov area was Sergei Schmierago, who played a vitally important role in our atrád's operational planning. Abrami Ivanov ferreted out information about the rail movements. Vanda, a woman of Polish origin, carried railway information to Kolya Gnedyuk, who directed the Zdolbunov cell. (Vanda now lives in Moscow.) She also obtained blanks of official German forms and passes for Kolya, who was a master forger. Vanda worked for about a year and a half as a courier in the Zdolbunov area before the Germans started to smell something. Then she was pulled out and brought to our central encampment. I learned all about this after the war, when Medvedev himself wrote his books. But when I was in action, I didn't know exactly how these train ambushes were prepared. Medvedev's first book was titled *The Strength of Spirit*, and his second book was titled *It Happened Behind Rovno*.

After my first demolition mission, I was in good spirits. We had accomplished something! The day after our return to our encampment, Commander Malik came over to me and said, "Well, Kohn, how did you like it? How'd it go? Afraid?" He obviously remembered how I had pestered him about getting into action. I answered, "I came to this group to be taken on missions. I asked you for action and I'm happy." He said, "I know, Kohn, . . . I know how you feel. We all feel the same way." This took place during the summer of 1943. We rested for five days, during which time another section of our group went out on a mission under the direction of Malik's second-in-command. (My section had gone out with Malik himself.)

Five or six days later we were sent out in a different direction. We lay for a whole night by the tracks, but we didn't blow up anything. The train we expected didn't come, so we went back into the forest. (We always picked ambush points where the tracks passed near forests.) We remained in the forest all day, and then, when night came, we returned to our trackside positions. We let one train pass, a second train too, and then a third. At five o'clock in the morning we blew up a train. This time we didn't have to divide ourselves into two sections, on both sides of the tracks, because there weren't many troops on the train; it carried ammunition to the front. This was all known before, and our plans had been prepared accordingly. We put three big mines under the tracks. These mines were controlled by us from the forest. (Sometimes we even manufactured our own mines, complete with timing devices. At other times we didn't need to use timing devices — the mines were detonated by pressure from the train.) This ammunition train was an enormous train. After we put the mines in position under the tracks, we were told to pull back to a point half a kilometer away. Although at the time nobody knew why, it was a wise move; when the train exploded and the artillery shells on board detonated, they created an enormous explosion. Anybody close by would easily have been killed. There certainly wasn't much left of the ammunition train.

For several months, such missions were our steady occupation. We came and we went, leaving havoc in our wake. The Germans saw that they couldn't easily counter our type of activity. What could they do? They instituted a new system of placing guards every 500 or 600 meters along the tracks. They took local peasants and made each of them responsible for a 500 meter to one kilometer section of the track. If anything happened on that section, the guard would be held accountable. What could such a guard do? He had a very loud whistle that gave off a piercing, reverberating echo. When he would whistle, a nearby guard would pick up the sound and whistle too, then a guard farther on would also whistle and spread the alarm, until the sound of the whistle came to a German guard post, which would quickly go into action. Airplanes would immediately be sent out in many cases. This was quite a system, although it sounds simple. The Germans couldn't establish it all the way from Germany to the front, a distance of 3,000 kilometers. But we were most active and best organized in the western Ukraine and in Byelorussia, so the Germans probably intended to concentrate on those areas.

We managed to overcome this system, however. After it had been established, our commander told me, "Kohn, today you yourself will place the mine in position. This is your assignment." They then briefed me in the atrád, although they didn't have to brief me much because all along I had been observing very carefully.

When we approached the tracks, we saw a guard standing there. We went another half a kilometer, or a kilometer, and there were more guards along the tracks. Three of us then moved in very quietly on one of them and grabbed him from behind so that he didn't have a chance to whistle. We gagged him, and then I dug a hole under the tracks and buried the mine. We divided our group into two sections, one on each side of the tracks, since we expected a troop train rather than a munitions train. To tell the truth, we preferred attacking troop trains because we liked to deliver the message to the Germans personally. Also, with a troop train we could capture booty we needed for the atrád, like machine guns, and various other weapons. Absolutely nothing could be kept personally by a partisan — all booty had to be turned in to the atrád's officers. This procedure was very strictly enforced.

Sometimes we captured a live prisoner. We never bothered to capture low-ranking Germans, but occasionally a senior officer would fall into our hands, and we would take him back to our atrád headquarters. Sometimes, when we attacked a troop train, one or two Germans would run out of the train in an extraordinary way: they were laughing rapturously, yelling joyously, and waving their arms in sheer, wild pleasure. At first, we couldn't understand what was happening. When we captured several of them alive, we discovered that they had gone completely crazy. They were in some form of hysterical shock. They met the same fate as their more normal German brothers.

The peasants who were guarding the tracks were not Banderovtsy. They had been forced into this guard duty. We investigated this matter *very* carefully — if they had been Banderovtsy we would have blown them away like dust. So, after gagging the trackside guard, we blew up the train; Germans ran out of it from all sides, and we mowed them down. The whole matter took no more than five minutes. We took the bound and gagged guard with us, because we had to find out what was really going on. We took him thirty or forty kilometers to our atrád, and we held him for several days. Our commanders sent people into his town to check out what he had told us. After our staff ascertained the truth, we let him go, but unfortunately, the Germans had already killed his wife and children as an "example" to other guards.

The Germans knew where we were, but they were afraid to come after us. We were not a little group. The partisans had such a widespread campaign that it was virtually a second front. We were in deadly and regular confrontation with those German beasts; it wasn't a matter of sporadic actions here and there. At least at the front the Germans knew the enemy that they were facing; here, in the "secured" hinterland, they didn't know when or where we would hit them, and we would hit very often. This kind of war must have been hard on their orderly and disciplined German nerves. In the Rovno Oblast there were 30,000 partisans, and partisans were never captured alive. They could be taken dead but not alive. Seventy percent of the partisans were former Soviet prisoners, who had escaped from the Germans. They had already been in German camps, and they would never again fall alive into German hands. They knew exactly what was awaiting them there, and they told the other thirty percent. I already knew. We also learned about German behavior from villagers who had escaped from some German mass slaughters. They explained in detail what the Germans were doing to innocent civilians, so we knew exactly how "humane" they could be.

We were in quite a quandary about those trackside guards. We didn't want their families to die, but we still had our important missions, which had to be carried out. We got around the problem in various ways. Once, our whole forty-five man group was sent out on a mission. It must have been

[115]

an extremely important train. The target area was quite far from our encampment, about sixty kilometers away. It took us a couple of days to get there. The guards, with their whistles and sticks, were standing beside the tracks. One guard came running over to us and begged, "Please, don't blow up my section! Hit another secton of the track guarded by somebody else! I have a wife and children! The other guard down the tracks is a bachelor, but I have infants at home. Please!" So we went over to the bachelor, and he started begging too; but we had a job to do. So we blew up a train, and then went another couple of kilometers and placed another mine under the tracks. We took the second guard back with us, but we didn't want this fact to become known so we spread the word that he had abandoned his post and run away. He remained with us and turned out to be a capable fellow.

A week later we were sent to Kovel. This was in another area, near Lutsk. Kovel was the location of a major railroad junction. We moved in on a trackside guard, and he started begging us, "Please — before you do your work, I have only one favor to ask of you. Beat me up very thoroughly! Knock the hell out of me! Make sure that I'm bleeding and all cut up. Tie my hands up and then do what you must do!" He wanted it to look as if he were forced. We acceded to his request — we beat the hell out of him. And then we proceeded with our mission.

As time passed, our work became more difficult. The Banderovtsy groups became bigger. A guard detachment had to be sent out with our group (or half the group) on each mission. We would have to pass villages, and in every village the Banderovtsy had their people. They prepared ambushes, and we often lost good men, usually two or three men during each engagement. It couldn't go on like that, but there was

[116]

no obvious, easy solution. Finally, when the demolition squad went out on a mission, we had to be protected by a whole platoon of infantry. A small number of men could have achieved the desired end of blowing up a train, but we had to have a sizeable escort. There was no other way.

One incident took place on a mission to a point just beyond Lutsk. We arrived without any harassment, and we blew up a train. We weren't engaged at all by the Banderovtsy, but on our way back, we fell into an ambush they had carefully prepared. We were twenty men then, and they were a full battalion — 300 men. (A battalion had 300 men, and a company had 100 men.) The battle lasted over an hour — a rare thing with the Banderovtsy, who usually ran away after five or ten minutes. We had three or four dead, and a half dozen badly injured, but we massacred this Banderovtsy group. Dawn was coming, and we had pushed them out of their initial ambush positions. They only had one way out, across a stream. When we came to the stream we saw that it was red. However, that was one of the worst engagements; it cost us good men.

We never left an injured man, or even a dead partisan, behind. The atrád had its own field hospital in the woods — that very same hospital where I was taken when I first joined Medvedev.

A number of the doctors ostensibly worked for the Germans in Rovno, and they were connected by messengers with our atrád. We took from the Germans all of the necessary medical supplies. Because of my weak condition when I first joined the atrád, I got to know the hospital very well. The medical care there was excellent. There were a number of general practitioners, but as the number of wounded rose, we needed more surgeons. Our staff learned that there was an underground group in Vinnitsa that wanted to join the partisans, and one member of this group was a professor of surgery. Our atrád needed him badly, although Vinnitsa meant a round trip of about 900 kilometers, often through hostile villages. Franz Ignatovich's wife was sent on foot on the difficult overland trip to meet this group. The trip took three weeks, and she returned with nine or ten men. One was the surgeon we so badly needed: a professor of medical research named Gulyanitsgog. Today he is one of the greatest surgeons in Leningrad, where he heads a great institute. He took over the supervision of all the surgery in our atrád.

Once, a certain atrád group had just returned from a mission, and they brought back one of their men who had been shot twelve times in the abdomen. I was walking past the hospital just at that time. Somebody emerged from the hospital tent and called me in. He told me, "Take off your rifle and wash your hands well; you will hold the patient's feet down during the operation." To tell the truth, although I had been in many battles, and was a seasoned veteran, I didn't think I would be able to look at an operation taking place. I told the doctor, "Let me notify my Commander." But he answered, "It's not necessary. I've drafted you for this operation because it's a severe emergency. The operation must be done immediately!" So I went in and washed my hands. They didn't anesthetize the patient — perhaps they were short of anesthetic. The patient was wide awake. The surgeon took out his intestines, cleaned them carefully, sewed up the wounds, and then closed the large incision. It took over two hours. I wondered how the hell this moribund man could remain alive! With twelve bullet wounds in his gut? There was a wet snow falling outside, and the operating conditions were very primitive — a raw wind kept blowing through the tent.

Two or three months later, amazingly, I saw the patient on his feet. He probably wasn't 100 percent healthy, but I saw that he would soon be well enough to hold a gun again. He would fight another day against the bloody Germans. I would never have believed it had I not seen the whole thing with my own eyes!

Every evening, the latest newsletter was sent to every group in the atrád, and the news from the front was read to all the partisans. We didn't have newspapers, so these bulletins were our only news from the outside world. They were typed by the atrád's radio operators who received daily news summaries on their radios.

I was in the demolition squad for five months. I was very happy there and got to know the members quite well. In the evenings, I used to walk over to various platoons and chat with friends. When I joined Medvedev's atrád, the atrád numbered 800–900 men; this number swelled later to 1,500. However, even then, there were rarely more than 800–900 men in the encampment. The rest were on missions. Nobody knew what the other groups or companies were doing. Nor did those going on missions know where they were being sent or the purpose of their missions. Nobody was told anything. Only when we came to our destination were we given our exact orders. We always saw groups coming and going, but nobody knew anything. Security was *extremely* strict. When I came back from my first mission, I was told, "What you did and where you were, you don't know. One wrong word and you will pay for it with your life. Security is very strict with us. Never forget that." Subsequent events demonstrated how necessary these security measures really were, because at certain times our atrád was infiltrated by enemy agents.

Once, in mid-morning, at the beginning of 1943, a terrible commotion arose in the encampment. I heard yelling, shrieking. Our men started to run to the source of the disturbance. I ran too; in one second, our normal routine had been broken by this sudden eruption. The yelling came from a man on horseback who had galloped into our encampment — he was blubbering and crying. When he calmed down a bit, he was brought to our commanders. I heard everything he said.

Our sudden visitor came from Pshebrazhe, a Polish village I mentioned earlier. The Ukrainian nationalists had surrounded Pshebrazhe during the night. They were numerous and well armed, and they tore into the village. They went about their "work" in a very orderly fashion: they went from house to house, slaughtering everybody. They took young girls, raped them in front of their fathers, drove wooden stakes up their vaginas (a typical Banderovtsy form of torture), and then watched them die. Only after the fathers and husbands had been forced to observe these atrocities were they killed too. Some were also forced to watch certain Banderovtsy who specialized in hacking off the breasts of living women and girls. The horseback rider had had to break out of the encircled village and ride fifteen kilometers to our encampment. This took time, and all the while the Banderovtsy were doing their terrible deeds.

In most villages, there were one or two people who were connected with our atrád. The Banderovtsy must have found out about our informant in Pshebrazhe, so they decided to launch an orgy of sadism, as was their custom. They preferred Jews as their victims, but Jews were nearly extinct by this time, so they had turned against the Poles; they even treated their fellow, non-Banderovets Ukrainians in the same sadistic manner.

When the Germans occupied the Ukraine, the Banderovtsy jumped on their bandwagon — they thought that they would kill the Jews and become the sole proprietors of the whole Ukraine. So, whenever Jews were slaughtered, four or five Germans would participate, "helped" by 100 or 200 Ukrainian nationalists. When the Ukraine became virtually *Judenrein* ("cleansed of Jews"), the Banderovtsy turned on their Polish neighbors. Pshebrazhe, a Polish village, was surrounded by Ukrainian villages and settlements. For hundreds of years relations were excellent between the Pshebrazhe Poles and their Ukrainian neighbors. They were even guests at each other's feasts and celebrations. Suddenly, centuries of friendship were erased and replaced by more than just murder — by a barbarity and sadism I could never have even imagined in my darkest nightmares. I couldn't understand it then, and I cannot understand it now.

Medvedev reacted very rapidly to the messenger's news. He sent two companies to Pshebrazhe, and I was among them. By the time we reached the village, 40 percent of the villagers had been slaughtered. We surrounded the Banderovtsy and repaid them well for their great deeds. They were really taken aback, these Banderovtsy. They had surrounded Pshebrazhe, and then they found themselves surrounded by us. Frankly, my heart wasn't entirely in this battle. The Banderovtsy deserved everthing they got, and more, but I had never forgotten that an independent Jewish group, led by an Ignatovka schoolteacher, had been betrayed by these same Pshebrazhe villagers.

When I had been with the demolition squad for five months, commander Malik came to me one day and told me to report to the command headquarters. I asked, "Why?" He said he didn't know. He told me to button up properly. My spoken Russian was quite weak then, so he told me, "When you come to the commanders, stand at attention and say, *"Tovarishch ofitzer, pribyl boyetz takoi, takoi, takoi. Po vashim rasporyazhenyiam."* ("Comrade Commander, Private So-and-

So from this and this group reporting for duty at your command.") Malik repeated this phrase with me fifteen times until he was sure that I knew it by heart.

I knew where the command staff was, although I had never been there. The staff was always in the center of the encampment. The hospital, the radio operators, and the command staff were always located together in one area. When I came out of the hospital during my first days with the atrád, I saw the commanders milling about. I didn't ask, but I saw that they were "biggies." So I knew, even then, that I was near the command and operational center of the atrád.

When I arrived at the hut that housed the command staff, I was stopped by two partisans on guard duty. It was evening. They asked me for the password, and I told it to them, explaining that I had been ordered to report to the commanding officer. They asked me where I came from, and I told them. I remained standing, and they went in. After five minutes, one of them came out and told me to go in. I went in, snapped to attention, and repeated my well-rehearsed words, "*Tovarishch ofitzer, pribyl boyetz . . .*" Medvedev told me, "At ease, comrade. Are you a watchmaker, a professional watchmaker?" I answered, "Yes, comrade commander, I am." He continued, "I have a watch to fix." He took out an extremely thin silver pocket watch. There was a two-letter monogram, in gold, on one side of the case. I needed a knife to open it, so Medvedev handed me one and I opened the case. I saw that the balance staff was broken. I might have been able to fix it, but I lacked the tools. I explained this to the commander, who said, "Look, we have many watchmakers in our atrád. I'm going to give you my adjutant, Sidorov, who will take you around to those watchmakers. You may take from them whatever you need, but I want to underline one thing: *This watch must be fixed!*"

[122]

Sidorov was called in. The problem was explained to him, and we set out to visit the other watchmakers in the atrád to see what they had. I needed to have a lathe or at least a drill to bore the balance staff. Sidorov and I went around for an hour and a half. Every watchmaker had hung on to some tool or part. They trembled over these treasures, but I guaranteed that I'd return the tools to them after I was through. However, what I really needed I could not find, so I told the adjutant, "I can't do the job because I need, at best, a lathe, or at the very least, a drill. And we haven't found either of these. Without them the job is impossible."

We returned to the command staff, and I told Commander Medvedev the situation. Medvedev looked at me with great intensity. He said, "Think it over very carefully. Examine the problem from all angles. *The watch must be fixed!*" I repeated what I had just told him — that it was impossible. He finally said, "Okay, you're dismissed, partisan. You may return to your unit."

When I returned to my unit, Commander Malik asked me what had happened, and I told him, He himself had not known the reason for my summons. At that time, one of our detachments was away on a mission, so things were quiet in our *tchoom* (the typical partisan shelter, a large, circular type of lean-to, not unlike a tepee). I thought most of the night about the broken watch that had been shown to me. I knew that, when our group went to blow up a train, we brought back booty, which often included watches. Other groups brought in even more booty than we did. Many times, on the way back from a mission, I was shown captured watches and asked about their quality. Many of those watches were of really superb quality. German officers seemed to have a particular love of fine watches. So I wondered why Medvedev was so insistent about fixing that particular, thin

[123]

watch. But then, when I remembered his tone and expression, I knew that whatever the reason, he wanted that particular watch repaired, and no substitute would do. But how could I fix it without the proper tools? I wracked my brain for an answer.

At night, an idea popped into my head. I would make a new part from scratch! It was such a farfetched idea that I debated with myself whether even to try. But Medvedev had made clear how important it was, so, after several days, I went to see my commander, who had just returned from a short mission. I explained to him that I wanted to see Medvedev again because I'd had an idea for fixing the watch. Malik told me that he would let the "biggies" know, and a short time later I was called to the command staff again. I reported as before, and when the formalities were over, I said, "Tovarishch commander, I'm going to try to fix the watch in an improvised way that may work. If it doesn't work, please don't be angry with me." Medvedev had very piercing eyes. I felt those eyes boring straight into me. He said, "Okay. What do you need for the job?" I answered, "I'll have to visit the other watchmakers again to collect what I need, and I must have a small bench, a small worktable, and a candle, all set up under a tree."

When everything was ready, I set to work. I took a small piece of wood, like a pencil, and I stuck a needle in the end of it. I sharpened the needle on a stone, and from this needle I made a drill. I used the candle to soften the steel of the staff, and I drilled a hole in it. I knew I couldn't make it perfectly accurate — it would be a bit off center — but I had no choice. Even the use of a candle to soften the steel was highly unorthodox. When I drilled a deep hole, I put in a piece of needle that fit very snugly in the hole. I smoothed the needle on a stone so that it should serve as a balance staff. I worked from

[124]

dawn till the evening; I didn't eat at all. The sweat was pouring from me.

When I finished, I returned to the command staff, but it took some time and explanation before they finally let me through. While I waited, I was so relieved, so happy, that I thought I'd surely give a yell of joy when I was admitted into Medvedev's presence. However, it didn't happen like that; when I went in, I became speechless. I just took out the repaired pocket watch and handed it over to him. I was utterly exhausted. He glanced at my face, then at the watch. He seemed to be rather serious, almost depressed. Then he looked more closely at the watch, and he saw that the second hand was moving! He put the watch to his ear and his face lit up. He exclaimed, "It's working! You did it!" I answered, "Yes, I fixed it." Medvedev came over to me, put his hand on my shoulder, and said, "You're quite a guy! Sit down and rest. You just did an extremely important thing!" Then he started a conversation with me. He asked me where I was born, where I had studied and worked. I think he knew exactly how I had joined the atrád, but he asked me all about it anyway, and I repeated my adventures to him. He shook hands with me and said, "Partisan, you may leave now." I left and walked back to my unit. After the war, I found out that this watch I had repaired was a key item in the disguise of our atrád's master infiltrator, Kuznetsov.

When I returned to my group, I was exhausted and tense. Malik looked at me and asked, "Kohn, things still aren't going well?" I answered, "No, everything's okay." So he said, "Then what's wrong? We can all see the nervousness on your face." I answered, "I've been concentrating all day. It was harder than placing a mine under a track!" Malik said, "Okay, Kohn, I understand. Tomorrow we won't take you along. You'll rest up." The weather had turned quite cold by

[125]

then, and he must have felt that I had been weakened a bit by the strain I had been under. I answered, "No, no — I want to go along with the group." But he insisted, "You're going to rest, Kohn, and that's that!"

The next morning, when I saw the men preparing to go on a mission, I begged Malik again, "Please! It's more of a rest for me to go with you than to hang around the encampment." I managed to talk him into taking me. We didn't go far, only twenty kilometers. However, on our way back, we were attacked by Germans and police. The train we blew up probably radioed the direction of our withdrawal. We had a considerable number of wounded, and it took a long time before we could break out.

When we finally did, we kept going for five or six hours, until dawn began to break. Malik ordered us to stop and rest until evening. We would move on when night came. As we were resting and full daylight appeared, the partisans all around me started to laugh — at me. I didn't see the joke. They called Malik over, and he laughed, too. He shouted, "Kohn, alive?!" I said, "Of course I'm alive. I'm talking to you!" I hadn't noticed that bullets had passed through my coat in many places. It was a bulky garment, and I wore it unbuttoned, so I hadn't noticed the holes. When I took it off, you could almost see through it. And yet not one of those bullets had touched me! So Malik said, "You're a *Vesuche* — (a 'lucky one'). I heard about your past adventures. No bullet can down you!" Afterwards, nobody called me Kohn. I was "the Vesuche." This was my nickname in the whole atrád from that time on. When we returned to the encampment, Malik took my coat and sent it "upstairs." Two men came — I had never seen them before — and one of them gave me a hearty slap of approval on the shoulder and said, "Your commander had good reason to name you 'the Vesuche.' You certainly deserve that name!"

[126]

We didn't go anywhere for a week after that; we were preparing ourselves. It was quite cold, but the trees in the forest seemed to make the woods warmer than the open fields. One day, our whole company, over forty men, was lined up. A closed pot was brought over, and a bit of liquid from the pot was poured into tin cans. (Those tin cans had held Lend-Lease preserves sent from America). Every man took a drink. Each man was given a piece of kielbasa (a type of sausage); we had a kielbasa maker in our atrád. This kielbasa wasn't usually given as part of the regular rations. It was given to partisans who had to go lengthy distances under severe winter conditions. With their own food supply, they wouldn't have to go into the villages and hamlets to obtain food, and they could thus remain unnoticed.

The lengths of kielbasa were measured with a string. My turn finally came; I was given a can to drink. I sniffed, and I knew that the stuff in the can was whisky. I had never drunk whisky in my whole life. I said, "I won't drink this stuff!" The commander then came over and said to me, "Kohn, listen to me. It's not summer now! We have to go a long way. We may have to dig into the snow for twelve hours. So *you have to drink* — that's an order! It's a matter of survival." I said, "To-varishch commander, I've never even tasted the stuff before!" He looked at me sharply and said, "Look, I've explained the matter to you. What's wrong with you? Are you still hanging on to your Mama's apron strings? I've ordered you to drink, so drink!"

Well, an order must be obeyed, so I smelled the stuff again — that was bad enough — and then I took a drink. Well, all hell broke loose! I never finished that drink. My eyeballs popped out of my head! I couldn't breathe! I was suffocating! I became congested, and a blackness filled my head. I didn't accompany my comrades on that mission. I was barely revived, and then they dragged me to the field hospital, where I remained for twelve days. My throat had been severely burned. I couldn't eat anything warm because my throat felt as if it were on fire. Messengers were sent from the atrád to nearby hamlets to obtain certain types of soothing drinks for me. I was living on cold milk. When I recovered, I was taken to the command staff, and they asked what had happened. When they heard, they said, "What, you never drank spiritus* before?" I answered, "What spiritus? I thought it was whisky." They said, "No, it wasn't whisky. It was our best spiritus, a type that can almost revive the dead. But in your case, it must have lost its sense of direction, and it almost worked the other way. You're a lucky fellow!"

I no longer went on missions with Commander Malik. My service with the demolition group ended at that point. I was transferred to the small group of partisans who served the command staff, and a whole new chapter in my life began.

* Super-refined vodka.

NAHUM KOHN

Nahum Kohn
and Howard Roiter

Aleksandr Fyodorovich Felyuk,
Partisan Commander

На долгого память
бывшему партизану
тов. Кон с первых
дней организации
партизанского отряда
декабрь 1942 г.
От бывшего
командора партизане-
кого отряда.
Фелюка Александр Ф.
Фелюк

Felyuk's Dedication for Kohn
"To comrade Kohn, my fellow-partisan from the very first days of our
Atrád in December, 1942.

From former Commander Aleksandr Felyuk."

КОМІСІЯ В СПРАВАХ КОЛИШНІХ ПАРТИЗАНІВ УКРАЇНИ

ПАРТИЗАНСЬКИЙ КВИТОК № *120*

Пред'явник цього тов. *Кон*

Кухен Якубович

в період Великої Вітчизняної війни був учасником партизанського руху і підпільних організацій

на Україні з *1 травня* 1942 р.

по *1 жовтня* 1944 р.

Голова районної
(міської) комісії

Дата видачі *2 лютого* 1968 р.

Kohn's Partisan Identification Card

Dmitry Nikolayevich Medvedev
Commander of the Atrád

Aleksandr Aleksandrovich Lukin
Medvedev's Second-in-Command

Nikolay Ivanovich Kuznetsov
("Hauptmann Paul Siebert")

Nahum Kohn in 1946

Lydia Lisovskaya

Valentina (Valya) Dovger

Dr. Albert Venyaminovich
Tsessarsky

Pyotr Mamonyets

Nikolay (Kolya) Strutinsky

Nikolay (Kolya) Prikhodko

Kohn, Mamonyets and Fellow Partisans
in the Tsuman Forests

Victor Semyonov

Mietek Stefanski

*In the Forest Where Gen. Pipper Was Defeated
Kohn (left) speaks to the partisans*

*Nikolay (Kolya)
Gnedyuk*

*Sergey Trofimovich
Stekhov
Commissar of the Atrád*

Vera Grebanovna

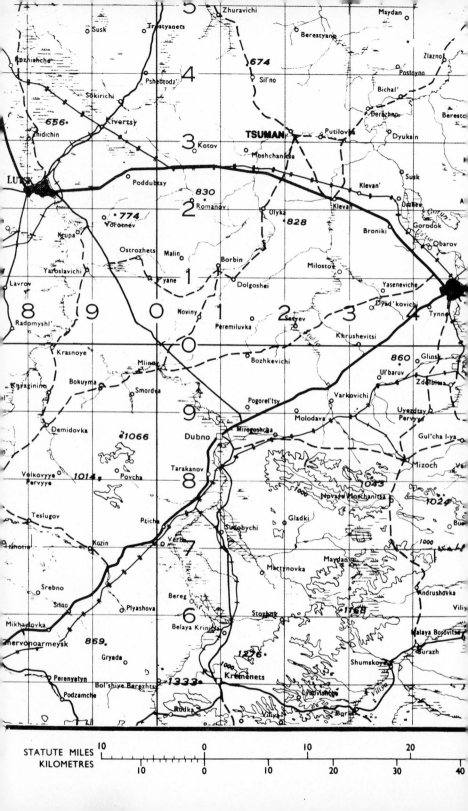

STATUTE MILES

KILOMETRES

10   0   10   20

10   0   10   20   30   40

PART FOUR

The small number of partisans who were attached to the command staff served in a support capacity, assuring the smooth functioning of our atrád's leadership. Although, as one of that small number of partisans, I was only a small wheel in the big machine that was Dmitry Nikolayevich Medvedev's atrád, I was at the center of things, since I served directly under the atrád commanders. I therefore could see and hear much relating to our atrád's operations. I had joined, or to be more accurate, fallen into the demolition squad at the beginning of 1943. It was summer when I was transferred to the command staff support group, and we were still based in the dense forests near Tsuman.

I have mentioned the accomplishments of Kuznetsov and the role he played in Medvedev's atrád. It would not be an exaggeration to say that the whole atrád was set up to facilitate and support the vital work of this one man. I had the privilege of helping this great man, in however small a way, witnessing some of his achievements. It pains me that, in the West, so little is known about Kuznetsov. He deserves more recognition than we can ever give him.

When Kuznetsov first joined the atrád, Medvedev and Maria Fortus (the atrád's chief of operations for a time) sent him, with Kolya Strutinsky's father as his guide, to Rovno for three days. The elder Strutinsky knew Rovno very well. He briefed Kuznetsov and familiarized him with every important location in Rovno: the Gestapo offices, the German General Staff headquarters, the German living quarters, the military warehouses, and the rest. Kuznetsov thus obtained a firsthand, exact picture of occupied Rovno.

Kolya Prikhodko, who had been dropped by parachute with Kuznetsov, was in charge of preparing a base for Kuznetsov in Rovno, a "safe-house." He came originally from Zdolbunov, twelve kilometers from Rovno, where he had been a member of the Komsomol. At the beginning of the war he had been evacuated into the Russian interior and trained intensively.

Kolya's work was cut out for him — he had to get going on it. He went with a group of men to a hamlet near Rovno to see his sister, Nasya, who lived there with her husband, Sergei Schmierago. Nasya became very excited when she saw her brother and quickly called her other brother, Ivan Prikhodko. He came, and he noticed that Kolya was accompanied by three capable-looking fellows. Ivan said, "Where the hell are you from? Did you drop out of the heavens?" He had thought that his brother was in the Soviet interior. Kolya answered, "Yes, Ivan, you're right! I did come from the heavens! I was dropped from the sky!" Ivan got the picture immediately and saw the reality behind the jesting banter. A "suggestion" was made to Ivan: a German officer, Paul Siebert, would be based in his house. Nobody was to know about Siebert and this arrangement. When the proposal was made, Ivan hesitated; he thought that the war was over and the Germans were installed in the Ukraine forever. But Kolya finally talked him into collaborating with our atrád. Kolya and Ivan were brothers, yet they were two very different human beings. We were lucky that Kolya had some influence on his brother, who lives in Rovno today.

Nobody in our atrád knew Kuznetsov's real identity. The

very few who knew him or knew of him called him "Grachov." A short time after Kuznetsov returned from his Rovno reconnaissance trip with the elder Strutinsky, he was sent there permanently, accompanied by Kolya Strutinsky. Kuznetsov, alias Grachov, alias Paul Siebert, was ready to do his work.

Kolya Strutinsky, dressed as a German, served as Kuznetsov's chauffeur in Rovno for over two years. He was really Kuznetsov's right-hand man. Strutinsky didn't speak German well, but the German army had in its ranks many Volksdeutschers (ethnic Germans), so Kolya Strutinsky for security's sake also pretended to be a Volksdeutscher. The Strutinsky family was really a decent one; Kolya's mother washed the partisans' clothes, while his father was responsible for food storage and allotment. George, Kolya's brother, was an expert machine-gunner. He had a special assignment in Rovno, which I'll explain later.

Kolya Strutinsky's mother met a tragic end. A big German airfield was located in Lutsk, and our atrád had to have one of our people employed there. We had tried to place somebody there several times, but it had never worked out. Mrs. Strutinsky, on hearing of one of these failures, spoke out and explained that she had relatives with connections in Lutsk. So she was sent to Lutsk, accompanied by her niece Yadga, her son Rostchik, and ten partisans. She met her relatives, and they helped her obtain a job at the strategic airport. On the way back from Lutsk, Mrs. Strutinsky and the others entered a house to rest. The house was surrounded by Banderovtsy, and a terrible fight ensued. Three partisans were killed and Mrs. Strutinsky was also killed. Her son Rostchik somehow survived.

When the group finally made it back to our atrád, a heart-rending scene took place. They had to tell the senior

Strutinsky that his wife, who had borne him nine children, had been killed. We were all affected by the murder of this kind woman. Medvedev said that this murder could not go unpunished — all the Banderovtsy who were in on it had to be repaid. Every single one of them — without exception. Kolya heard about Medvedev's reaction, so he reported to our command staff and begged for an assignment as the leader of the group that would be sent out to punish the Banderovtsy. Our commanders refused even to consider Kolya's proposition — his own mother had been killed, and his feelings could override his judgment. He was too involved in a personal way. Kolya's pleading was not successful, but he was allowed to go on the punitive mission as an ordinary partisan. I was not sent on this mission.

Our commanders sent 120 men, under the command of Valentin Semyonov, on this mission. They didn't leave a single member of that Banderovtsy group alive. A river ran through the area, and when the criminals tried to escape through the rushing water, it soon turned red with their blood. The battle started at 4 o'clock in the morning and lasted until seven. Over a hundred Ukrainian nationalists fell there. Mrs. Strutinsky had been avenged, but this vengeance could never restore her to us. Our world has all too few decent people like her, and we really felt our loss.

Although I emphasized the fact that Kuznetsov killed many senior German generals, his main assignment was the gathering of military intelligence. For a year Kuznetsov confined himself to this task. He set up networks of reliable and efficient informants. As the year wore on, Kuznetsov saw that, with our growing strength in Rovno, more could be done. So he told Medvedev and Lukin (who had replaced Maria Fortus) that the time was ripe for ridding the earth of those vermin. He couldn't just stand aside and see what they were doing every day to innocent people. Kuznetsov gave

Lukin and Medvedev the names of the most nefarious German generals, including that of General Ilgen, a bloodthirsty butcher. He was responsible for the "disposal" of all people living in the Ukraine who were deemed to be anti-German. Jews, of course, were his prime interest.

Medvedev and Lukin couldn't give the go-ahead themselves — they had to ask Moscow for permission. After a time, when Kuznetsov was in the atrád encampment for some business, Medvedev told him that Moscow had approved the killing of a general, but not General Ilgen. Another general had been named. Kuznetsov wanted an explanation, but Medvedev said that Moscow was clear on this point: Ilgen's time would come later, *but he was not to be killed now.*

Although disappointed about Ilgen, Kuznetsov was overjoyed with this qualified go-ahead. He could finally start collecting the debt these assassins owed to humanity. From this time on, the personal "diversions" started. Kuznetsov first killed the Special Military Commander-in-Chief, Colonel-General Kietzinger.

Our atrád had sixteen radio operators, who kept our communication lines open on a twenty-four hour basis. Our commanders decided that one of our operators, a woman, should be based in Rovno because communication on foot took much too long. She would maintain direct contact from Rovno to our encampment, and Moscow could even transmit direct instructions to her for our Rovno-based agents.

The radio operator, Valentina Konstantinovna Osmoilova, was dressed like a typical Ukrainian peasant woman, although she was a Russian. She was accompanied by Kolya Gnedyuk and Kuznetsov, and they traveled in a wagon covered with hay. The bulky radio apparatus was covered by the hay. They had hidden two automatic rifles under the seat, as well as several grenades.

They covered the sixty kilometers from our atrád to

Rovno, and all went well. The horses, however, were raised in the forest; they had never been in an urban area before. As the wagon approached the Rovno Bridge in the center of the city, two cars were crossing the bridge from the opposite side. Our horses became terribly frightened; they reared up and started to run. They didn't run far, however, because the wagon flipped over on its side, and the radio and automatic rifles fell onto the pavement.

The two cars, filled with German soldiers, came to an abrupt stop. Kuznetsov, however, did not lose his cool-headed control. He was wearing his German captain's uniform. He walked straight over to the Germans and started to scold them. "Fools, what are you staring at? We've captured a partisan bitch and all her equipment, and all you dummies can do is stare? C'mon — help me right the wagon!" This was an order. They all ran over and pushed the wagon back on its wheels. They put everything back in place, and then saluted and left. Kuznetsov, Kolya, and the radio operator then drove to Ivan Prikhodko's house, which was to serve as the radio base. Kuznetsov's cool control had saved the day, and it was not the last time that this self-control was to save both himself and his colleagues.

All of this happened in February or March of 1943. The radio operator worked in Rovno for ten days, but the Germans quickly established that radio messages were being transmitted from a certain part of town. Our people didn't think that the Germans could find out so rapidly, but they seemed to have special electronic detection equipment that we were unaware of. The Germans set out to check the area where Ivan's house was located. But Kuznetsov, working among the Germans, knew that Ivan's area would be checked, so he had the woman and her equipment moved from the house. The Germans came, checked, and found nothing except a grouchy Ukrainian, Ivan, who seemed to be sympathetic to their cause.

After several days, the radio operator was brought back to Ivan's house. The Germans again picked up the radio signals flying through the air. They had the area pinned down but they didn't know which house was serving as a transmission base. Once, in the evening, two SS men came to check the house. One of our men, serving as a lookout, saw them coming, and this gave our operator time to shove the radio apparatus under the bed, get undressed, and jump into bed.

When the SS men came in and saw a uniformed German captain in the house, their attitude changed immediately. The SS men explained why they had come: to find an illegal radio transmitter. Kuznetsov commended them for their devotion to duty, and explained that there was no chance of hiding a radio in that house, under his very nose. They checked each room and finally came to the bedroom that was used for the radio transmissions. They saw a woman in bed, and they immediately asked about her. "Who's this woman? She could be a bandit!" Kuznetsov kept his cool as usual and answered, "Ah, she's only a local whore I picked up several blocks away. Boys, we have to keep our morale up! If you guys want a piece of the action, I can cut you in!" And as he said that, he pulled the cover down and showed them the naked woman. Kuznetsov continued, "C'mon, guys! You only live once!" One of the SS men answered, "Sir, we can't. We're on duty. Thanks anyway." They slammed the door, went downstairs, and left the house.

After this incident, the radio operator was ordered to return to the atrád. She had been lucky, but the next time her luck might run out, and Kuznetsov would not be there to bail her out. As a result of the atrád's failure to establish a radio base in Rovno, the commanders decided to move the atrád encampment from a point 130 kilometers from Rovno to Berestyany, which was only 70 kilometers from Rovno. Radio contact between our encampment and Rovno had proved too risky — we needed couriers or messengers to maintain contact with our Rovno-based agents. Our atrád's outposts were located at the halfway point between our encampment and Rovno.

At the beginning, our chief courier was Kolya Prikhodko. In my opinion, he made one of the most important contributions to the success of Medvedev's atrád, although we lost him early. Kuznetsov obtained a base in Rovno through Kolya Prikhodko, and this base, Ivan Prikhodko's house, was essential for Kuznetsov's further work. Ivan's wife had a German mother, so she was officially recognized as a German, and Ivan was recognized as a Volksdeutscher. There could be no better cover than a Volksdeutscher's house — it was beyond suspicion. It is difficult to imagine how important such a cover could be in those times.

When people looked at Kolya Prikhodko, they became frightened. He was very tall, six and a half feet in height, with broad shoulders and a very serious face. But he was a generous and friendly person. Although he didn't have much formal education, he was a naturally refined person. It was very hard to find shoes for him because his feet were so large, and at times he had to go around barefoot.

Kolya was, at times, sent on missions that he could have accomplished himself. However, three or four men were always sent with him, because Kolya had one great weakness: when he saw a Banderovets policeman, he lost all self-control and threw himself on the nationalist. A Banderovets in front of Kolya's eyes was like a red flag in front of an enraged bull. The men sent with Kolya on these missions had one simple function: to keep an eye on him and make sure that his hot temper and enthusiasm didn't launch him into undesired adventures.

Once, our commanders sent several men with Kolya on a mission, and they made Seredenko the head of the small group. They came into a small hamlet and saw two Ukrainian policemen standing there. Kolya ran over to the two policemen and killed them right there. Seredenko said, "Kolya, I'm the leader of this group! You must follow orders!" Kolya replied, "How could we let those two go on with their terrible work. They're worse than the devil himself! They must be eliminated!" Our leaders knew about Kolya's hotbloodedness; they lectured him, scolded him, and tried to explain that his behavior could bring great trouble, but those Banderovtsy were a virtual obsession with him — he just couldn't stand the sight of them.

I believe that Kolya's obsession definitely contributed to his untimely end. He died very heroically, but unnecessarily. Things could have turned out differently. As I said, when Kuznetsov was working in Rovno, Kolya was the first courier connecting him with our atrád commanders. He traveled like a peasant, with a horse and wagon loaded with hay and farm produce. He took on a package, dropped off a package, and it all looked quite innocent.

Once, however, traveling back from Rovno with a very important message from Kuznetsov for our commanders, Kolya had to drive over the bridge at Tuchin, a bridge that spanned the Styr. As he approached the bridge, two Ukrainian policemen stopped him and asked to see his papers. Kolya pretended to reach for them, but instead he grabbed the two policemen and banged their heads together. He stunned them and grabbed their rifles. Here he made his fatal error: he could have killed them then and there, but he forced them instead to climb up on the bridge railing and jump into the cold, fast-flowing Styr. The bridge was high above the river, and the drop was a considerable one. The river currents were strong, and Kolya figured that the two policemen would drown. After he forced them to jump, he looked down and thought that they had gone under.

Kolya kept going, but, unknown to him, the two policemen survived. They must have been good swimmers. They immediately phoned the nearest German post and gave an exact description of Kolya. Kolya continued for six or seven kilometers past the bridge, and then he ran into trouble. The Germans had prepared a roadblock — they were very efficient in such matters — and as the horse and wagon came around a bend, Kolya saw a car blocking the road. He couldn't go back because a car had moved out on the road behind him. So Kolya left the road and drove the horse and wagon across a field for several hundred meters.

The Germans started to fire at him, and they first hit the horse. Without the horse, Kolya couldn't get very far. He used the dead horse as his cover, and he carried on the fight from a prone position between the horse's outstretched legs. It was a very lopsided battle. Kolya was all alone and completely surrounded by the Germans. He had been wounded twice and had used up almost all of his ammunition. He saw that his situation was hopeless — they were trying to take him alive. They might discover important things if they could capture him. So, badly wounded as he was, he took out all of his important papers and burned them to a crisp. Then he took a grenade and blew himself up. He killed twelve Germans and injured quite a number of others in that battle.

The loss of Kolya was one of the most serious losses that our atrád suffered. Everybody liked him; he related to people on a personal level. The fact that he had been killed was not immediately made known by the atrád commanders, probably for morale reasons. After Kolya's death, Kuznetsov moved from Ivan Prikhodko's house to that of Vale Burin.

After the war, Kolya Prikhodko was posthumously declared a Great Hero of the Soviet Union, just as Kuznetsov was. In Zdolbunov, at the railroad station, there is a big monument of Kolya holding a grenade, ready to explode it and blow himself up.

Much has been written about Kovpak's atrád, for one very simple reason: his was the largest partisan atrád in the whole war. His work was diversion — to make a lot of noise; and they did make a lot of noise, blowing up tracks, warehouses, garrisons. That's why Kovpak's atrád became so well known. Ninety percent of Kovpak's activities were in Carpathia.

Kovpak had his successes and failures, and at one point his atrád was ordered to rest, preferably in a forest where there would be other atráds nearby. Near Medvedev's atrád there were many others — in Rovno Oblast alone there were 30,000 partisans. So Kovpak's atrád moved toward Rovno, to rest in the Tsuman forests.

Kovpak's atrád numbered over 3,000 people. When they moved, over a hundred people moved a kilometer or two ahead of the main body as an advance guard — and they were all dressed in *German uniforms*. We did not know that the advance guard moved in this disguise, and our ignorance nearly led to a disaster. As they approached us, our partisans manning the outposts saw a whole army of German soldiers moving in on the atrád. The outpost personnel instantly notified our atrád commanders, and the alarm was given; an immediate state of high alert was instituted.

In a short while, Kovpak's men were battling with our outpost people, who couldn't hold out very long against such a force and therefore fell back. A very hot firefight followed. The combatants were in a forest, very close to each other and firing away, when a miracle took place. Boris Krutekov recognized that one of the "Germans" had studied with him at an artillery school before the war. Boris knew him very well. At the same time, Kovpak's man recognized Boris, so he started to yell, "Boris! Boris!" Boris responded by calling the "German" by name, and shouting out, "What in hell is going on here?" The "German" answered, "We're Kovpak's men." So each of them ran back to his own side and explained the matter. White rags were hoisted and the shooting ceased, but all of this took 10 to 15 minutes. There was great joy at that time, because they had all been a hairbreadth away from disaster. Indeed, before the shooting stopped, Kovpak's commissar (his right-hand man) was wounded, and seven or eight other men from his atrád were badly wounded. I believe that one was even killed.

Kovpak brought his whole atrád into our encampment. Our commanders met with him. Kovpak said, "I've heard a lot about you guys — in espionage and infiltration you are tops! But I didn't know that you can fight like tigers too!"

Kovpak's commissar was treated, with the other wounded, in our hospital, and Kovpak made an unusual request. He said, "We've heard legends about the feats of your German. Permit me to see him! We've heard all about his great accomplishments." Medvedev didn't answer immediately; he took some time. Perhaps he radioed Moscow about this request. Anyway, the next day Kuznetsov was recalled from Rovno, and a dinner was arranged in Medvedev's hut.

Those present at the dinner were Medvedev, Stekhov, Lukin, Kovpak, the commissar, and one other of Kovpak's team. Kuznetsov came into the hut resplendent in his German uniform. Medvedev said, "Here is our German, Grachov." Kovpak said, "I can't speak with him. I know no German." Medvedev said, "Don't worry — I think he knows

[142]

Russian too." Kovpak's commissar said to Kovpak, "We do what every atrád does, but we do it on a bigger scale. If we would have this Grachov . . . Ah!" They ate, spent some hours together, and then they separated. Kovpak had had his treat — he had seen the German.

The fact that I was a watchmaker was generally known in our atrád. Once I was called into the commander's room (I usually was stationed just outside, or close by), where I saw Medvedev and Lukin sitting together. Lukin said to me, "Kohn, how would you feel about being sent to work at your trade in Rovno?" He took me completely by surprise when he said that — I just didn't expect it. A thought quickly flashed through my mind: Is this a time to sit and fix watches in a civilian shop? Meanwhile, Medvedev spoke up: "This is an extremely important matter." Since I hadn't answered anything, Lukin continued, "If you feel that you don't want to go, you can refuse. We're not giving you an order now — we're just asking you how you feel about the idea." So I asked, "Exactly what kind of work would I be doing in Rovno?" Lukin answered, "I want to send you to Rovno to work in a shop as a watchmaker; in Rovno, you would find out more about the job. If you were not a Jew, Kohn, we'd order you to go. However, since you're a Jew, and the job would be particularly precarious for you as a Jew, we're giving you the right to refuse." The commanders were being quite realistic, I thought. I said, "If the job is a necessary one, then I'm ready." Medvedev said, "Okay, but go back to your quarters, think it over carefully, and give us your final answer tomorrow."

I reported to the commanders the next day and told them that I was ready for the mission. If it was necessary, I felt, then it had to be done, and that was that. I really didn't have to agonize over my decision. They then told me why they were sending me and just how risky it was. Lukin said, "It's a very risky mission for two reasons: you are going to be an information drop deposit point for our agents in Rovno, where one of our people will serve as your intermediary; second, you're a Jew, and to be a Jew in Rovno now is . . ." He didn't have to complete the sentence — I knew what he meant, and yet, in prewar days, Rovno was 90 percent Jewish. Lukin continued, "In several days, somebody will come for you from Rovno. He knows all about you. He's been briefed very carefully. He'll get to know you, and then we'll discuss a few things."

In two days, the "somebody" came; his name was Ivan Kutsenko, and he worked as a watchmaker in Rovno. He was an intelligence intermediary for our atrád. As I stated above, Rovno had been 90 percent Jewish before the war, and virtually all of the watchmakers had been Jews. They had all been murdered by the German beasts, so Rovno badly needed a good watchmaker. Ivan Kutsenko had a watch repair shop there, but he wasn't a professional watchmaker; he was an amateur who had graduated from a technical school as a mechanic. In his spare time he used to play around with watches. Our atrád needed to have somebody who would do real watch repairs for the Germans — an amateur bungler could attract too much attention. We did have some five or six professional watchmakers (non-Jews) in our atrád, but the commanders selected me for this mission.

Ivan Kutsenko and I got to know each other, and he briefed me about the job in Rovno. He explained that very few civilians would come in to the shop; 80 percent of the clients were Germans and Ukrainian policemen, or members of the Ukrainian SD (Ukrainian Security Forces — they still operated at that time). These customers would be interested in rapid repairs, since they needed the watches for their work. After several days, I got to know Ivan very well. Then I was called back to the command staff, and they took over a month to prepare me for the job. All aspects of my future behavior and reactions were drilled into me. I would be living as a Pole under the alias of Mietek Kowalski. My Polish accent was perfect. Because I came from the Polish heartland my Polish was much better than that of a Pole born in the Ukraine. My cover as Mietek Kowalski was logical because at that time there were some Poles living in Rovno — not many, but there were some.

I was awakened in the dead of night and told to report immediately to the commanders. There I was given a nice suit, shirt, and tie and practically new shoes; these clothes felt very odd on me because I hadn't worn a suit and tie for a number of years. I even laughed at myself, strutting around like a peacock. Dressed up like that, I was supposed to remain unseen by other atrád members; nobody was to know that I was dressed like that. I was taken out of the commanders' hut into the pitch black night and brought to Rovno. (Since I served the commanders myself, I knew that this was standard procedure in top secret missions.)

Before my departure, Kuznetsov spoke to me for several minutes. I rarely saw him personally in Rovno; I received his messages from Ivan Kutsenko. I had been briefed to the point where, even if I should run into somebody from the atrád in Rovno, I wouldn't bat an eyelash — I wouldn't know him and he wouldn't know me.

When I arrived in Rovno, all of my papers were in order. They showed that I had already been living in Rovno for a number of months. Ivan Kutsenko remained with me for a week. He showed me how to deal with the customers, what the procedures were, and so on. After two or three days, two men came with Ivan Kutsenko, and they told me that we would be going to the movies that evening. Believe me, I really didn't feel like going to the movies. Rovno was crawling with human vermin — the whole German general staff was based in Rovno, not Kiev. The Germans had made Rovno their capital because they figured that it was far from the front and full of their allies, the Ukrainian nationalists.

We walked slowly down the streets and looked at various billboards, notices, and advertisements. We entered the movie house and watched a German propaganda film about the great exploits of the "racially pure" Aryan supermen. We had to leave early because there was a curfew in force: a civilian couldn't be out past a certain hour. Believe me, I breathed easier when we returned to my shop after this expedition.

After several days, Ivan and his companions visited me and told me that they had a treat for me: we would be going to a restaurant. When we entered the restaurant, I noticed that there were no civilians there, only German soldiers. I saw how Ivan and his friends were watching me: they wanted to see how I would react to all of this. Believe me, I was tense, but this "treat" came off well, as did several other trips to the movies and some long walks to the local market. Later I found out that they had specially selected German propaganda films to check my facial reactions. After a while, I had been so well trained that I myself forgot that I was a Jew. I swallowed my alias completely: I was a veteran resident of Rovno, familiar with all the streets, movies, restaurants. At that point, my training period was over; Ivan Kutsenko left, and I started to work on my own.

I worked in my shop for several months. I regularly received and forwarded intelligence information. My German clients were relatively easy to handle; I fixed their watches in two or three days, they picked them up and paid me, and that was that. I had hidden, near my workbench, two small grenades, and I carried a pistol. In case of an emergency, I was to make sure that I would not be taken alive. Some weeks after I started working, I noticed, from behind my counter, that two men on the street were keeping an eye on me. I had never seen them in the atrád, but I was told that they were "our's." They didn't maintain a steady surveillance, but I would see them drift occasionally across my line of vision.

I had one very close call. I couldn't stand my Ukrainian nationalist customers. I could control myself in movie houses, restaurants, and markets, but when those Ukrainian policemen came in I almost lost my control. Many times, when I opened the cases of "their" watches, I saw a Jewish monogram on the case. I used to wonder: had the watch once been a treasured Bar Mitzvah gift from a proud father to an only son? And where were they now, both doting father and Bar Mitzvah boy? Some of those Ukrainian policemen wore three or four wristwatches on each arm, and I knew the origin of those watches, how they had been "obtained."

Once, a senior policeman came into my shop and said I had to repair his watch while he waited — he needed it urgently. (I'll never know why it was so urgent if he had so many others!) So he was standing around while I worked on his watch. Meanwhile, two junior policemen came in with their watches lined up on their arms, and they struck up a conversation with the senior policeman. They explained how they had come by each of those watches. What an explanation that was — it turned into vicious boasting about deeds against innocent Jews, and those deeds were so cruel as to make my hair stand on end. Death is one thing, but sadistic torture is another matter, and those Ukrainian policemen boasted about the slow, painful, and gruesome deaths they had especially devised for "their" Jews. I couldn't continue

[147]

listening to their words, so I stood up suddenly and reached for the grenade hidden under my desk drawer. I caught myself just in time, however. One policeman said, "What's wrong, watchmaker? Did the watch fall down?" I answered, "No, only a part fell, but I found it already." I had regained my self-control just in time.

I saw that my nerves were shot — I couldn't take it any more. So I asked to be allowed to return to the atrád for several days. After a week, I was told that the commanders had decided to grant my request, and I was taken back to our encampment. I went to see Lukin and told him, "Please, pull me out of Rovno!" He asked why, so I explained, "Comrade Commander, I can't stand it any more. When they come in and take three or four watches off each arm and I can see Jewish monograms inside the cases — this I can take, although it's hard. But when they start to explain how they tortured this or that Jew before killing him — the sadism is beyond words! My sanity can't hold out any longer! I can't take it!" Lukin took it all in, and then said, "Listen, Kohn. Your work for us in Rovno is much more important than laying a mine under railroad tracks, or battling Germans and Banderovtsy. What you are doing in Rovno is a hundred times more important for our atrád and for our whole work. Take a rest, and then we'll take you back to Rovno." I said, "Please, let me stay another day or two in our atrád. I want to recuperate a bit more among our own." They let me stay for another three days, and I shortly calmed down and regained my composure. Then I was brought back to Rovno.

While I was recuperating, Kuznetsov killed a senior German general in Rovno, right on the street. He was the financial councillor of the Reichskommissariat of the Ukraine, General Doctor Gehl. This assassination was a mistake, however. Kuznetsov was supposed to kill another general, not Gehl. Valya Dovger, one of our atrád's most outstanding agents and a person of whom I will speak extensively, had told Kuznetsov that this other general, who always carried a yellow briefcase, would come out of a certain restaurant with his adjutant at a specific time. This general was twenty minutes late. Meanwhile, Gehl, carrying a yellow briefcase, left the restaurant in the company of his adjutant, Colonel Winter. Kuznetsov killed both Gehl and Winter, and at the scene of the "crime" he left certain documents and five or six gold pieces. These documents showed that a Ukrainian nationalist, who had been sent from Germany by Bandera, had assassinated the two German officers. The German SD examined the documents and passcard, and they drew the "proper" conclusion: they rounded up the Ukrainian nationalist leader in Rovno, and they tortured him. I believe that they finally shot him. And in Rovno the German-Banderovets love affair, which was already weakening, turned into a feud.

The day after the assassinations, Kuznetsov came to our atrád. Valya Dovger brought a newspaper that told how the finance minister and his adjutant had been killed. Only then did Kuznetsov learn that he had made a mistake and killed the wrong man. He was taken aback by this newspaper article, but Medvedev put his hand on his shoulder and said, "Don't worry! It's not such a big mistake. We should all make such mistakes!"

Our Rovno agents ran into some trouble while I was working as a watchmaker. Vera Grebanovna is today an instructor in the central committee headquarters of the Rovno Communist Party. When I worked as a watchmaker in Rovno, she was an eleven-year-old child living with her mother, Kulikovskaya, one of our agents in Rovno. Her mother, among her other duties, provided our agents with a safehouse in Rovno.

Once, as I was walking to work, I heard shooting coming

[149]

from the general area of the Rovno Bridge (a small stream goes through Rovno). I became apprehensive. The noise turned into the sound of explosions and heavy rifle fire; I also heard the sound of grenades exploding. I kept on walking to work, but my heart was heavy, and with good reason. I later found out what the commotion was all about.

German counter-intelligence had discovered that Soviet partisans were being sheltered in Kulikovskaya's house, so they surrounded the place. The German information was correct; there were three of our men in the house at that time. These three men battled the numerous, heavily armed Germans for over three hours, and then they retreated into the crawl space under the roof and continued the battle from there. By the time they only had a few bullets left, one of them had been killed, and the other two were wounded. These two knew that they had no chance of emerging alive from the Germans' clutches, so they shot each other to avoid falling alive into the enemy's hands. The Germans succeeded in capturing only corpses; our men had burned all the documents and incriminating papers. Eighteen Germans were killed by our atrád's three men, and many more were wounded. Several Banderovtsy were also killed during the battle.

The Germans then picked up Kulikovskaya, who was 28 years old. She was tortured terribly for ten days — the German animals needed no lessons about sadistic, bloodcurdling torture techniques — until only a quivering mass of flesh remained. She was then hanged. She was an extraordinary person — a warm, humane woman who did good deeds that were not known even in our atrád. She hid a young Jewish student named Fishbein, from Sarny, in her house. (He lives in Israel today.) She hid Fishbein for a lengthy time, and he taught Vera how to read and write. When the Germans attacked the house, Fishbein, by sheer luck, was not there. Vera's mother had taken him to her best friend for several days — she probably felt that something was in the air. Fishbein, up to this very day, corresponds with Vera Grebanovna.

The Germans often sealed off streets and made spot checks, but this was not the cause of the attack on Kulikovskaya's house. Somebody in her family — a brother or a cousin — collaborated with the Germans. I had seen such a thing before: the same family, one person behaves like a real *mensch* and another turns into a beast.

I continued my work in Rovno; I was already into my fourth month on the job. Once I noticed a boy hanging around my shop. He looked as if he were eleven or twelve years old. I had a little display window in which I kept a cuckoo clock for advertising purposes. When, later on that same day I decided to rearrange the display a bit, I again noticed that boy loitering outside the shop. I started to feel uneasy.

The next day the boy reappeared and, after much hesitation, came into my shop. He saw that I had a client just then, so he quickly went out. I saw him near my display window, and several hours later he came into the shop again. I was quite suspicious by now — perhaps the Germans had found out about me and that meant . . . The boy said, "Uncle, maybe you can show me where the partisans are?" I almost jumped out of my skin! I figured that the boy must have been sent in by the Germans. I ran over to the window and looked out, but I didn't see any Germans. Then another thought flashed through my mind: the boy must have been sent by the Ukrainian nationalists. However, I saw outside only the two men who were hanging around to protect me, as usual. I turned back to the boy and said, "Get out of here

[151]

before I give you partisans in your rear end! You have the nerve to go looking for dirty bandits?" I picked him up and wanted to start beating him, but he started to cry. He pleaded, "Please, please tell me where they are!" I reflected a bit and said, "Well, what do you need partisans for?" The boy answered, "I must see Medvedev's atrád." Well, that took the cake — the kid was looking for my own atrád! The matter was becoming more complicated by the minute. I asked again, "What do you need the partisans for?" And the boy was again tight-lipped; he just repeated, "I must see Medvedev!" I said, "Come tomorrow at one o'clock, and I'll take care of your problem." The boy then left my shop.

In the evening, I saw Ivan Kutsenko, and I told him about my young visitor. He already had heard about the boy from the two watchers outside the shop, but when he heard what the boy had said he took off like lightning to tell Kuznetsov. Ivan soon returned; Kuznetsov had told him to give me a specific order: when the boy appeared for our 1 o'clock appointment, he was to be detained until Kuznetsov himself came into the shop.

The next day, several minutes before one, the boy arrived. I started to talk to him, I told him to sit down; I pretended to be busy; I went off to look for a part in the back. The boy refused to be put off; he continued to pester me about the partisans. I said, "Wait until I finish this job — then I'll tell you everything." He noticed that I was stalling, and he became suspicious and frightened. He started to shift about nervously on the chair.

Just then, the door opened, and a German officer (Kuznetsov) came in. I said, "Herr Hauptmann, this boy is looking for Medvedev's partisans." When the boy heard this he started to cry and stammered: "No, no . . . I wasn't looking for partisans." He made a dash for the door, but Kuznetsov

[152]

was too fast for him, and he grabbed the boy. The boy tried to pull himself loose; he was yelling and howling. A car pulled up to the shop, and Kuznetsov shoved the boy into the car, which immediately sped off. Ivan Kutsenko then came into the shop and said, "Forget about this. Keep on working!"

I worked in Rovno for an additional three or four weeks. Then I was recalled to the atrád, and when I was back at our encampment did I learn the sequel to my adventure with the young boy. The car had carried the boy and Kuznetsov off to one of our outposts, and the men there had brought them to our encampment. The boy was taken to the command staff, and Kuznetsov explained the whole matter to Medvedev and Lukin. They asked the boy who he was and why he was looking for partisans. The boy saw that he was now in the woods, among partisans, so he took off his hat. A coded letter had been sewn into the lining. Then he took off his pants. In the seat, another coded message had been concealed. Only Lukin and Medvedev could decipher the messages. When Medvedev read them, he embraced the boy and said, "Take a good look at this kid! He went five hundred kilometers on foot. His father sent him to find us, and he found us!"

The boy, named Kolya Smerov, came from a small 120 man atrád operating near Vinnitsa. His father was the leader of the atrád. However, there was a traitor among them, and the whole atrád was destroyed. The only survivors were the father, the boy, and one other partisan. They had lost their radio operator, so they no longer had contact with Moscow. (This was the only other atrád controlled directly by Moscow; it had been dropped near Vinnitsa because something very big — we didn't know what — was going on there among the Germans.) The father knew that Medvedev was operating near Rovno, so he had no alternative: he sent the boy 500 kilometers to find Medvedev, and the boy had accomplished his goal. Our atrád didn't return the boy to his father — it was too risky. The boy remained with us. Medvedev radioed Moscow, and Moscow parachuted several men into the father's area; they explained the matter to him.

The father had told the boy only that there were many Medvedev partisans in Rovno — nothing more. The boy wandered through the streets of Rovno, examining the location of the Ukrainian SD offices, German police stations, and so on. I worked in an area relatively distant from the Ukrainian SD offices. The boy, during his wanderings, saw a watchmaker's shop with a cuckoo clock in the window — this clock fascinated him. He saw people going in and coming out of the shop, so he hung around, hoping to chance on a clue. He had hung around other shops too, but without any success. As he was looking at my window display, two of our men left my shop, and one said to the other, "Listen, this is an order from Medvedev!" When the boy heard that, he realized that he had found his destination.

I worked in Rovno for five months. Our luck, however, began to turn sour. We had several failures. Kulikovskaya was hanged, our three men in her house were killed, and George Struthinsky was captured alive (I'll have more to say about George later). One day my contact man came into my shop; he was edgy, and he told me that my mission in Rovno was over. I was evacuated the next day, but I have never been able to fathom the precise motives behind the termination of my mission. My opinion is that the Germans found out that the watchmaker was connected with the partisans. It would seem that I had been recalled to the atrád just in time — we were half a pace ahead of the Germans. Our commanders wouldn't have evacuated me for nothing. If things had been quiet, I would have been replaced, at least, by Ivan Kutsenko. But nobody replaced me — it was too hot.

My watchmaker's shop in Rovno had provided a drop for intelligence information. Some of the information left with me was carried to the atrád by couriers; one was a fearless little twelve-year-old boy, Kolya Yanishevsky, Kuznetsov's special courier. For a year and a half, this boy covered, three times a week, the forty-kilometer round trip between our encampment outposts and Rovno. This young courier was nicknamed "Little Kolya" in our atrád, and he played an extremely important role in our atrád's operations. He came originally from Klosov, where his father was a stonemason. His mother had been killed by rampaging Poles.

In Rovno, little Kolya's bases were Vale Burin's house, as well as Maria Levitskoi's home. When he used to arrive at these places, he would wash and change his dusty clothes, but Kuznetsov didn't allow him to leave the house. He sat inside, day after day, listening to the adults' conversation. Kuznetsov, after several weeks, saw that the child was suffering; he was being confined like a prisoner. This bothered Kuznetsov, so he hit on an idea: a chum must be found for Little Kolya.

The chum turned out to be Romka, Maria's 10-year-old son, who had been boarding with relatives. The boys were introduced, and they struck up an instant friendship. They became pals.

Several months passed. Kuznetsov once bought a small harmonica for Kolya, who loved to play simple tunes on it. On one occasion, Romka wanted to borrow it, but Kolya refused to lend it to him. Romka quickly lunged forward and tore the harmonica out of Kolya's hand. When Kolya finally managed to grab the toy back, Romka was sobbing, and he blurted out, "Wait, I'll show you, you lousy partisan!"

An elderly man, Marchuk, lived in that building. He was a secret policeman employed by the Germans. Marchuk heard Romka's exclamation, so he grabbed the boy, while Kolya scurried away. Romka was petrified; everybody was afraid of

Marchuk. He shook the boy and yelled, "Where is the partisan? Who is a partisan?" Romka replied, "I was just joking . . . I didn't mean it." Marchuk, however, was adamant. *"You are going to tell me what you know!"* He started to drag the boy to the police station for interrogation. He wanted to know where the boy had picked up the word "partisan." The approved word, which was widely used by the Germans and their Ukrainian allies, was "bandits," not "partisans."

Romka howled so forcefully that the neighbors came out. A chorus arose in the yard. "Marchuk, let the child go! He's only a kid!" One woman said, "Leave him alone! We all know that Maria's son is a good boy!" When Marchuk heard that, he dragged the boy into Maria's apartment. When he saw Maria, he demanded, "How does your boy come to mention partisans? What connection do you have with such vermin?" Marchuk took a quick look at the interior of the apartment, and to his surprise he noticed a German officer (Kuznetsov) sitting in the kitchen. Maria answered; "What partisans? I know nothing of such people!" The German officer stood up and came into the room. "Who's talking about partisans?" he said. "What do you mean by coming here to look for partisans?" Marchuk, taken aback by the appearance of this tough-talking German, answered, "I just heard this kid use the word 'partisan,' and I wondered where and how he had picked it up." Kuznetsov said, "Look how stupid you make us look! You should be chasing real criminal partisan bandits, and instead you go after kids. I don't blame you — you're dumb. I blame your superiors — what kind of men could have appointed you to a responsible position?" Marchuk, quite abject by now, answered, "I'm sorry, Herr Officer. I goofed." Kuznetsov said, "Okay, I'll forget about such foolishness this time, but you won't be let off next time, believe me!"

Marchuk left in a great hurry. Kuznetsov then asked Maria about this sinister man, and she told him all she knew. "He lives in this building and works for the German secret police. Many say he's from Odessa, but others believe that he's from Carpathia. He himself says he was born in Rovno and was an important accomplice of Petlura."

When Kuznetsov left, Marchuk returned to Maria's apartment. This time he was quite deferential in his speech. He asked, "How do you come to be on such familiar terms with a German? He's so polite to you! You really know each other, eh?" He leered as he said this. Marchuk continued, "Cultivate this German. If I get on his good side, I can really go places in my work. C'mon up to my place. I have the best food and drink. I'll do you a favor in return for your efforts on my behalf with that German." Maria ate and drank with him and told him that she would put in a good word for him.

Our atrád leaders were briefed about this Marchuk and young Romka's adventure. Marchuk was visited by our agents shortly thereafter, and he disappeared. I don't know the details of his end, but he had come too close for our comfort, and he paid for it with his life.

George Strutinsky, at the beginning of 1943, had been sent to Rovno on a special mission: he was to contact Soviet prisoners and incite them to escape from the Germans. Many Soviet prisoners, emaciated and maltreated, spent their days on the "outside" doing various jobs involving hard and dangerous labor; at night, they were returned to the prison compounds. For several months George was quite successful. He managed to send us groups of ten and twenty men. He used to send them to a contact point (a *mayak*) outside the town, and from there they were sent to another point before they were transported to our atrád. These former POWs turned into extremely good partisans — they were very devoted. Seventy percent of the members of our atrád were former POWs. They had been exposed to German cruelty, and each and every one of them had resolved never again to fall alive into German hands.

In May of 1943, George once contacted a group of prisoners, and he made an appointment to meet them near the Rovno Bridge. One of the prisoners, however, was a collaborator, and he informed the Germans about the proposed meeting. When George approached the bridge at the appointed hour, he was shot at, hit in the chest, and seized. He received that chest injury as he tried to reach for a grenade; he was one of the very, very few partisans to be captured alive.

Our atrád commanders tried to learn of his whereabouts, but they hit a blank wall every time. It was as if he had been erased from the face of the earth. Usually, he told somebody when he was about to go to an appointment, but this time he hadn't had the time to tell anybody; the appointment had been made only an hour or so before it was to take place. You can imagine how Kolya Strutinsky felt; he had lost his mother, and now his younger brother had disappeared. Several months passed, and our atrád still didn't know what had happened to George Strutinsky. Kuznetsov systematically "examined" every German and Ukrainian prison including those of the Gestapo and the police, and he finally discovered that George was in a certain jail — and still alive. He found this out through one of Kolya Strutinsky's contacts, a woman who worked as a domestic for the Ukrainian SD. She gave Kolya a carbon copy of the prisoner list. The Germans had kept George alive because they thought they could still extract information from him. They had tortured him for several months and given him painful injections, but George was an extremely strong person and had managed to survive.

When our commanders found out that George was still alive in that jail, Lukin prepared a plan to get him out. Lukin decided that one of the people of our atrád, officially registered as a Rovno resident, would have to infiltrate the Ukrainian police force. Kolya Strutinsky's cousin, Pyotr Mamonyets, had all of the qualifications for this job. He had once been a Polish army officer. He was connected with our atrád, but he was not based at our encampment. He lived in Rovno. He was called in, and the mission was explained to him: only he could save his cousin George. Mamonyets was given exact instructions — he was to become a Ukrainian policeman of exceptional caliber. He was to rise rapidly in rank and gain the complete confidence of the Ukrainian SD. His loyalty was to be absolute to them. Money was no problem — he would have all he could use to help in obtaining promotions, and the like.

Mamonyets followed his instructions, and his rise in the Ukrainian police force was meteoric. In a short time he was allowed to enter the jail and requisition prisoners for hard labor assignments. On one of these jail visits, he made eye contact with George.

Mamonyets once had a particular police assignment to fulfill on the outskirts of town. Certain ruins had to be cleared. He took two junior policemen, and they selected ten prisoners from the cells. Mamonyets managed to select George as one of the ten. After several hours on the job site, a car drove up, and a German officer emerged. Mamonyets ran over and saluted the German. They talked together, and the German pointed to George. "I'm taking that bandit with me for further interrogation. You have to accompany us." So Mamonyets went over to the two policemen and told them, "I'm leaving you with the prisoners; let them work until evening. I'll return soon, after I've brought this bandit in for further interrogation." George was shoved roughly into the car, and Mamonyets sat down. The German officer told the chauffeur to drive off. Only then did they notice that the chauffeur was George's brother Kolya. You can imagine how George felt at that time: to have been snatched like that from the jaws of the Nazi monsters.

Kolya Strutinsky drove the car straight to Mamonyets' house to take his son and wife away. When the Germans investigated the escape and linked it with Mamonyets' disappearance, his wife and son would pay for the escape with their lives. However, when our car arrived at Mamonyets' house, they discovered that the wife and son had already been evacuated by another group from our atrád under the leadership of Misha Shevchuk, who operated under the cover of an official agent of the Ukrainian SD. As an additional cover, he was also a part-time businessman. (He lives today in Lvov.) So, when our group reached the atrád, the joy was great! George was reunited with his relatives, and Mamonyets saw that his wife and son were in safe hands.

George was an iron man — only he could have withstood such interrogation. He was in bad shape when he was rescued, and Mamonyets was really lucky that no one questioned his selection of such a battered man for hard labor. George explained to us later that he remained alive because he had promised to cooperate with the Germans. He told them that he was a member of Saburov's atrád and gave them various invented locations of Saburov's encampment. When his claims were investigated and found to be untrue, he maintained that the atrád must have moved off. George's skin was blue from the injections he had received; his torso was covered with enormous, ugly welts.

I mentioned above that Mamonyets' wife and son had been evacuated by Misha Shevchuk. Misha lived in Rovno under the alias of Boleslav Yankevich, and he worked as a Gestapo agent. He was supposed to have come from Warsaw. Kuznetsov was amazed when he first saw Misha in Rovno. Misha wore an elegant suit and a black top hat, and he always carried a small bouquet of fresh flowers, even though he was not high ranking when Kuznetsov first met him in Rovno. Kuznetsov told him that, with a small moustache, he would have made a perfect Charlie Chaplin.

Misha was dreadfully feared in his Rovno neighborhood. He had a diabolical appearance, and he later took to wearing dark glasses. He would appear to be nonchalant, but he would peer into every nook and cranny, asking seemingly innocuous questions that could bring great disaster. Misha was such a perfect actor that he once came within a hairbreadth of being killed by our agents.

One of our partisans based in Rovno, Mazhura, once came to Maria's apartment, which he used as a drop for intelligence material. As Mazhura was sitting at the kitchen table, he saw that somebody was approaching the apartment. Maria hid Mazhura and his friends in another room; there was little time to spare before the little Charlie Chaplin figure came strutting through the door. He went into the kitchen, washed and shaved, ate a meal, dawdled over his tea, and then left. He used to love sitting at Maria's table and gossiping.

Mazhura emerged from the other room and asked Maria who the visitor was. She explained that he was a secret Gestapo agent who used to visit her often. Her neighbors were terrified of this diabolical dandy. He used to date her on occasion. Mazhura and his friends, that day, couldn't leave the apartment because the Charlie Chaplin figure was hanging around in the front yard. Four o'clock passed, then 4:30, and Mazhura and his associates were still stuck. The curfew hour for civilians, 5 P.M., was approaching. Finally, ten minutes before the hour, the agent went back into the apartment, spoke briefly to Maria, and they left together.

Several days later, many of our Rovno infiltrators were called back to the atrád encampment by Lukin. They were to be briefed about important new developments. Lukin used to like to debrief our agents separately, all the while going into great detail. He used to ask what street or lane was crossed during a certain operation, and then he used to explain that another street or lane should have been used. Everybody thought that he was a native of Rovno, but the truth was that he had never even been in Rovno.

Mazhura was one of our agents who had been recalled to the atrád. Kuznetsov had been recalled too, as were Kolya Gnedyuk and others. Mazhura asked to see Lukin to make a special request. When he saw Lukin, he said, "A terrible parasite lives near Maria and frequents her apartment. He hangs around her yard. He's a rodent of a man with a deadly face. He's a Gestapo agent, and this vicious vermin must be crushed! Please, give me permission to finish him off! He's dangerous!"

Lukin asked, "Mazhura, what did this agent ever do to you?" Mazhura replied, "To me he has done nothing so far, but people say that in Warsaw he uncovered large underground resistance groups. He did such a magnificent job for the Germans that he was brought specially to Rovno to continue his nefarious career! His eyes are always poking around behind those dark glasses, and even Ukrainian SD men whom I know fear him." Lukin again asked, "What, concretely, has he done to you? If he has done nothing, then perhaps it's better to have him live near Maria. He provides a good front for us." Mazhura then told how he had had a close call at Maria's, and how he had almost been spotted by the Gestapo agent. Mazhura said, "Why Maria receives him so hospitably is a mystery to me! Perhaps she's up to something behind our backs."

Lukin looked at Kuznetsov, and Kuznetsov looked back at him. They knew who the Gestapo agent was. Lukin said to Kuznetsov, "Have you heard about this agent?" Kuznetsov answered, "Yes, I've even met him. He seemed to be a decent fellow. Let's leave him alone. For us he's a good 'cover.'" Mazhura became livid at this point — his eyeballs were bulging out of his head. He said, "Of course, to you he's a decent fellow! He's on his best, most affable behavior for a German officer. But for us he can be deadly. And he will be deadly! Comrade Aleksandr Aleksandrovich Lukin, please! He's not a big fellow. We'll strangle him and place his corpse in a sack. He'll disappear from the face of the earth, and it won't even cost us one bullet."

Lukin, by this time, was smiling a bit. He asked Kolya Gnedyuk for his opinion. Kolya said: "Let him be. If he disappears, the Germans will start a room-by-room search, and who knows where such a search can lead? Leave the bastard alone." Mazhura was insistent, "I stand by what I said. Now that he hangs around Maria's, sooner or later he'll spot us." While they were talking, the door opened and the "terrible parasite" came in. Mazhura got terribly excited and started to yell, "Ah, here he is! Here he is! That's him! He's a double agent — he's working for both sides!" As Mazhura was yelling, he saw Lukin's smile and Kuznetsov's grin. The whole truth suddenly dawned on him. He was then introduced to that "terrible parasite," Misha Shevchuk, and they all had tea together while they enjoyed a good laugh.

When Kolya Yanishevsky was in our encampment, he used to play with a ten- or eleven-year-old boy, Pinya. Pinya was everybody's favorite in our atrád; we used to give him candies and various treats, because his manner of joining us was unique.

When Kuznetsov was in our encampment, he used to wear a large cape, which covered all of his body. Nobody was to know that he operated as a German officer. Thirty men in the atrád knew him as Grachov; only three men knew that he was really Kuznetsov. Lukin and Medvedev would often take Kuznetsov for short walks in the woods surrounding the encampment. While walking, they would plan the next operation and discuss relevant matters. Once, as Medvedev and Kuznetsov (Lukin was busy elsewhere) were walking in those woods, they heard an unfamiliar sound. Medvedev said to Kuznetsov, "Did you hear something?" Kuznetsov said he hadn't heard anything, but as they listened they did hear a sound, somewhat like a moan or a weak cry. Kuznetsov said, "Yes, I hear it. It's probably a small animal, or a bird." Medvedev and Kuznetsov then grabbed their revolvers, moved apart, and began a systematic search of the area.

In a short time they found the source of the sound — a little boy who was really hardly more than a skeleton. He was emaciated. His eyeballs protruded, his cheeks had collapsed, and his hair had fallen out. He could hardly move. His feet had rotted — he couldn't stand up. He was able to tell them who he was. His name was Pinya, and he had escaped a mass slaughter of Jews in a nearby hamlet. He was once a little Jewish boy, and now he hardly resembled a human being.

Kuznetsov was very deeply affected. He took off his cape, wrapped the boy in it, and carried him back to our atrád hospital. Kuznetsov told Lukin, "How could such a thing happen? I understand that war means killing, but how could anybody do such a thing to a small child?" His voice was choking with emotion, and Kuznetsov never — except for this moment — allowed his voice to express even his strongest feelings. His self-control was virtually complete, but the sight of this skeleton pushed him beyond that self-control.

Kuznetsov was supposed to leave for Rovno the very next day, but he had been shaken by this experience, and he asked for a delay of several days. The delay was granted, and Kuznetsov spent the next days in our hospital, nursing Pinya and encouraging him. Kuznetsov said that when the war was over, he would adopt Pinya as his own son.

Pinya was with our atrád for over a year. Whenever somebody came to our encampment from Rovno, he brought a message for Pinya from Kuznetsov. Pinya's health improved slowly, and the skeleton soon became a playful and cheerful youngster. Our men used to bring him clothes, food, and medicine.

Kuznetsov once came to our atrád commanders with a special request. He explained that Pinya came from a small hamlet of semiliterate and illiterate people. He wanted Pinya to learn — to receive a proper education and make something of himself. He wanted to have the boy sent to a special school in Moscow, and he explained that after the war he would join Pinya in Moscow.

A request made by Kuznetsov was something special. And Kuznetsov had made this request as a father concerned about the future of his own son. As a result, an airplane that brought us ammunition and other things carried Pinya on its trip back to Moscow.

Kuznetsov never saw his Pinya again. After the war, I asked Lukin about the boy, and he told me that an uncle in America had located Pinya and had brought him to the United States. I don't know where Pinya is today; I never even learned his family name. But I really wish I could see him now, to find out what became of the poor little skeleton Kuznetsov took into his very own heart.

Most people believe that the turning point of the war took place at Stalingrad. However, researchers have shown that the Germans' back was broken in mid-1943, near Kursk-Orel. Whoever won that mighty battle would gain an irreversible momentum. The Germans had assembled, for this decisive counterattack, an immense force totaling thirty-five divisions, under the command of Field Marshal von Manstein, Colonel-General Heinz Guderian, and Field Marshal von Kluge. For this operation, which they called Operation Citadel, they had organized a mighty armored force to serve as a spearhead. The German counterattack turned out to be a dismal failure, because the Soviet military leadership, headed by Marshals Rokossovsky and Zhukov, knew all about this massive counterattack long before it took place. The famous spy "Lucy," Rudolf Rossler, played an important role in providing this information. Kuznetsov also had a key role in this matter because vital information about the planned operation fell into his hands by accident several months before that decisive engagement.

In April of 1943 Kuznetsov was supposed to kill a monster, General Koch, the Nazi Gauleiter of the Ukraine. Koch was very, very hard to get at. His operations center was located in a Rovno building that had been a Soviet high school in prewar days. (Now it serves as the Communist party headquarters building in Rovno.) Even high-ranking Germans had difficulties if they wanted to see Koch; they had to have a special pass from very high sources. So our atrád commanders had to devise a plan that would get Kuznetsov into Koch's office.

About 100 to 150 people from our atrád were working in Rovno, in various capacities, ostensibly for the Germans. One of them was Valya Dovger, who came from the Sarny area. Her father was a senior forest supervisor connected with our atrád. The Banderovtsy discovered this connection quite by accident. They seized him, cut him into small pieces, and put him in a barrel. They were really sadistic murderers, these Banderovtsy — they didn't just kill. Dovger's daughter came to our atrád and explained that she wanted to avenge her father. She was then about sixteen years old and spoke perfect German because her father was of German descent. Lukin saw that this girl had special talents, so they trained her for several months. They introduced her to Kuznetsov, and she was sent to work as a courier in the documentation secretariat of the German Gebietskommissar.

Valya Dovger pretended to be Hauptmann Paul Siebert's fiancée. (The façade soon became reality, because a strong relationship did develop between them.) Valya ostensibly had had to flee from her home town because Soviet "bandits" had killed her Volksdeutscher father. Her father had been killed far from our atrád, and the Banderovtsy had poor communications between their groups, so Valya's cover was reasonably safe. In any case, she would have been hard to recognize. She had blossomed into a beautiful young woman. Her hairdo and clothing had been changed. Valya Dovger's main work consisted of "borrowing" certain essential documents from the Germans for Kuznetsov.

There was a severe labor shortage in Germany, so many people were sent to Germany to work in munitions factories. They were even sending Volksdeutschers to Germany, and one day Valya Dovger received her "greetings" letter instructing her to report for transportation to Germany. Valya went to Kuznetsov and showed him the letter. He saw in the letter exactly what he had been waiting for — the perfect excuse to meet General Koch. Kuznetsov returned to the

[167]

atrád encampment and, in conjunction with Lukin and Medvedev, worked out a plan.

Kuznetsov struck up an acquaintance with Gauleiter Koch's kennel master, the man who was responsible for Koch's dogs. Kuznetsov and the kennel master, who was a junior officer, would get together socially, and on one occasion Kuznetsov explained that a disaster had befallen him: his fiancée was being shipped off to Germany. Kuznetsov said that only Koch could do something about this — perhaps the kennel master could help by arranging an audience for Kuznetsov with General Koch. The kennel master, in expectation of a nice "tip" for his efforts, arranged an appointment for Kuznetsov. (This kennel master was chronically short of money, and Kuznetsov often "loaned" the officer small amounts.)

Kuznetsov killed high-ranking German officers with a silencer-equipped small revolver. It made no noise whatever. So Kuznetsov planned to kill Koch in his office, when they were alone together. Our commanders sent Kolya Gnedyuk and Valya Dovger with Kuznetsov on this mission. Kolya drove the horse and carriage, and he was supposed to wait for Kuznetsov in front of the building. In the carriage Kolya had concealed two submachine guns and several grenades. If everything went as planned, Kolya, Kuznetsov and Valya would drive away together. If a problem developed, Kolya was supposed to lob his grenades into the building and try to escape in the confusion.

Kuznetsov and Valya were not called in together to see General Koch. They waited ten minutes, and Valya was called in. She remained in Koch's office for five or ten minutes, and then she was escorted out by Koch's adjutant, a colonel, who told Kuznetsov: "Okay, now it's your turn." And he looked at Kuznetsov as if he pitied him.

When Kuznetsov came into Koch's office, he saw that Koch was sitting at this desk. Behind him were two SS men with submachine guns held in a ready position. Near Koch were two trained attack dogs. Kuznetsov was told to sit down, and Koch started to lecture him: "How could a German officer have the nerve to mix into the proper functioning of the Reich? How could he stoop to get involved with a Volksdeutscher's private affairs? The Reich needs people for essential work at home. She must go." So Kuznetsov answered, "I love her. I've loved her for a long time. Her poor father was assassinated by the Soviet bandits, and since then she's been doing useful work for us here." Koch shook his head in disbelief, "I can't understand it — such nerve! To expect the Reich to adjust its needs to your own private life!"

Kuznetsov's cover was that he had been sent from the front to take care of various matters. Koch knew his division, his commanding officer, and other details. So Koch asked him, "How is our boys' morale at the front?" (The Germans had taken a bit of a beating by then.) Kuznetsov answered, "Everything is in order. Our morale is high." Koch then asked him where he was born, so Kuznetsov gave him the name of the Prussian town where the real Paul Siebert had been born. Koch became excited, and explained that the town Siebert had just mentioned was his own home town. When he heard who Siebert's father was, he warmed up considerably and said, "Ah, I knew him well at school." They discussed the family estate, and Koch asked about a certain park; Kuznetsov explained that he used to play there as a child. Kuznetsov described the park in minute detail, and Koch enjoyed every moment of the description. He warmed up considerably towards this upstart "nervy" captain with the bold request.

Kuznetsov, on entering the office, had been told to put his hat down. He was sitting rigidly. He was told to put his hands on his lap. Whenever he moved his hands, even slightly, the dogs immediately stood up — that's how they had been trained. Kuznetsov made many attempts to move his hands, and each time the dogs stood up. So, Kuznetsov thought, only one option remained; as he left the office, he would whip out his pistol and kill Koch. That was the only way it could be done. He knew that he would probably have to pay for this with his life, but he thought that the sacrifice was worth it.

Koch, after the reminiscing, asked Kuznetsov when he was returning to the front. Kuznetsov gave him a date, and explained that he would return again to Rovno. So Koch said, "Since you're my *landsman**, I'll tell you something very special: the Führer has prepared a real party for the Soviet vermin! We will introduce new weapons to the world — Tiger tanks, Panther tanks, and Ferdinand self-propelled tank-like artillery. Those Russkis are really going to get it!" Koch excited himself with his own words; he named other equipment, and expostulated at length and in detail. He said that on a certain day the most massive counterattack in history would begin, a counterattack that would crush the Soviet war machine for all time! It would be the final battle of the war. This battle would start at Kursk (the immediate objectives being Olkhovatka, Ponyri, and Nikolskoye), and Koch even told Kuznetsov the day the attack would begin — July 5.

Kuznetsov was taken aback by what he had just heard. This information was much more important than Koch's death — it had to be transmitted immediately. Kuznetsov abandoned his plan to kill Koch, since the whole course of the war might depend on his new information. Koch told Hauptmann Siebert that he would be allowed to keep his fiancée in

* Someone who comes from the same town.

[170]

Rovno; Koch would personally cancel her travel order. So Kuznetsov rejoined Valya in the anteroom, and they went out together. He couldn't talk then, but when they got into the carriage, both Kolya and Valya demanded, "Did you do it?" When he said that he hadn't killed Koch, Valya said, "God, what happened? You chickened out?" Kuznetsov explained why he had aborted the plan. He had hit on information that was much more important than Koch's death.

Kuznetsov had left Koch at 11 A.M. By noon he was back at his Rovno base, and by 2:30 the news had been coded and radioed to our atrád. By 3 o'clock it was retransmitted to Moscow.

Kuznetsov, through his friendship with a German, Captain von Babach, later managed to obtain important technical data about the new equipment that would be thrown into the battle. This data was in Moscow's hands a considerable time before the actual battles started. Military historians have also noted that some months before the attack, the partisan attacks on the railroad lines behind the German Army Group Center tripled and quadrupled. This was called "The Battle of the Rails," and it began when partisans blew up the 330-yard-long bridge over the Desna on the Bryansk-Gomel railway line. German supplies got to the front with great difficulty, and the troops became somewhat demoralized.

Hitler personally briefed his senior officers about the strategic importance of the decisive counterattack that would shortly start. The Soviets, however, under Rokossovsky and Zhukov, were ready. The German attack timetable was wrecked. Where they expected two or three lines of light defense and then clear sailing — a breakthrough — they found six or seven lines of heavy defense. The German attack was contained and then repulsed. There were fifty days of uninterrupted intense combat over an area of 26,000 square kilometers, and thirty German divisions were destroyed. The Germans lost 500,000 men in this engagement, the greatest counteroffensive in history, and they were never again able to mount a significant counterattack against the Red Army. The Kursk battle determined the final outcome of the war, and its importance has been underlined by postwar researchers.

Almost every day prisoners were brought into the atrád — German or Banderovtsy. Of the 1,500 men in our atrád, 30 or 40 percent were usually out on missions. One of these groups, in July 1943, returned with a prisoner — a German gendarmerie major. The German gendarmerie played a particularly dirty role in assisting the SS in roundups and executions. They "policed" the whole process.

Prisoners were always brought directly to the command staff for processing. We guarded this one for over an hour; then the commander of our detachment, Fraire, a Spaniard (there were twenty of them in our atrád), said to me, "Kohn, take this prisoner to our place" — we had a field where interrogations took place. I didn't know who would question the prisoner; I was responsible only for guarding him and preventing his escape. When I took him to the interrogation field, his hands were bound behind him, I sat him down on a tree stump.

After waiting there for ten or fifteen minutes, I saw the man I knew as Grachov (Kuznetsov) approaching. When the major saw him, he turned red. "*Mein Gott,*" he said, "how does a German officer come to be here?" Kuznetsov went over close to him and asked him what his name was. The major ignored the question and said, "You're a traitor! How could a German like you cooperate with such Slavic scum?" Kuznetsov answered, "I'm not a traitor; I'm a Soviet officer." The major cried, "No, that's impossible!" Then he got angry and burst out, "You tied my hands up! That's not permitted according to the Geneva Convention. You call this fair play and decency? Is this your kind of justice?" Kuznetsov answered, "You want justice? You want fair play and decency? When you burn thousands of villages, and bury children and old people alive in mass graves — then you don't think of justice, do you? Look around at the man guarding you — he's a Jew. With us, all are equal. How can you even talk of justice, much less demand it?"

Kuznetsov asked the prisoner about his identity, where his unit was stationed, and what he knew about the airports and military units in the vicinity. Kuznetsov got out of him all he knew; the interrogation took about forty minutes. When it was over, the major asked, "What are you going to do with me?" Kuznetsov answered, "You'll be shot in half an hour." The major said, "I have only one thing to ask of you. Please — I'm from Berlin; I have a wife and two children — let me write a letter to them." Kuznetsov said to me, "Naum, untie his hands." He gave him a large sheet of paper, a pencil, and a lit cigarette; then Kuznetsov left. The major said to me, "He must have fooled me, eh? He can't be a Russian — no, that's impossible — he must be a German!" I answered, "He told you the truth. He is a Soviet officer." I want to underline the fact that Kuznetsov spoke to him for forty minutes and told him he was a Soviet officer, and still the German wouldn't believe him. That's how good Kuznetsov's disguise was.

The major wrote for about an hour. Kuznetsov returned and took the letter; the German took out of his pocket a photo of his wife and two children and gave it to Kuznetsov for inclusion in the letter. Ten minutes later it was all over; the Nazi officer paid for his "heroic" deeds against women, children, and old men.

[173]

The various partisan atráds had different functions. Kovpak's atrád was involved in diversionary activities; they made a lot of noise by blowing up bridges, attacking German garrisons, and the like. They tried to keep the Germans off-balance, and they were successful — the partisan war against the Nazis was virtually a second front. Our atrád had a different function; we were an intelligence-gathering atrád, and we specialized in military espionage. The Germans knew about us, and that is why they called in their anti-partisan "hit man," General Pipper. He was to destroy us completely.

The Germans tried to infiltrate our atrád with spies, mostly Ukrainian nationalists. Our atrád leaders caught almost all of them and finished them off. But we had one failure — a bad one. One of their spies, Nauminko, managed to become a member of our atrád. He was a former Soviet war prisoner of the Germans who had been "turned around" by them. He was with us for over six months. His rota (company) woke up one morning, in September of 1943, and discovered that Nauminko had disappeared. They searched high and low for him without success. Several days later, one of our spies in Rovno said that he had seen Nauminko there.

Valya Dovger had been working as a courier for the Germans, and she often carried important documents to the generals' homes. Once, when she brought some papers to the nefarious General Ilgen, he complained to her that he was about to receive an important visitor and he needed a hostess to help him. He explained that he was helpless in the kitchen, and his assistants had even less domestic ability. She answered that she wasn't much of a cook, but he said, "Your face is enough! Please help me — I'm in a bind!" So Valya remained in his house, and while she was puttering around in the kitchen, Ilgen said, "I have digestive problems. I've tried to hire a housekeeper, but I've had no luck. Those I like the Gestapo doesn't like, and vice-versa. Someone like you would be perfect. Or perhaps you could recommend somebody." Valya promised that she would look around for Ilgen.

At that moment the bell rang and General Pipper came in. Pipper's specialty was anti-partisan warfare, and his division had an impressive track record. Two crack SS police regiments, trained in Berlin, formed the core of his division. He had been successful in Yugoslavia, France, Czechoslovakia, and Poland. Then he was brought to Carpatho-Ukraine where he fought Kovpak's partisan atrád, one of the largest atráds with 3,500 men. Pipper almost completely destroyed Kovpak's atrád; Kovpak was evacuated by plane to Moscow, but his whole general staff was killed, including his second-in-command. (Pipper was nicknamed "The Minister of Death to the Partisans".) Kovpak was later parachuted again into the forests, and he started from scratch, so his atrád was finally a completely rebuilt one.

The Germans knew that all of the assassinations of high-ranking German officers in Rovno came from Medvedev's atrád. That is why they made a special request to Berlin for General Pipper. Ilgen was overjoyed when he received Pipper at his home. Valya Dovger heard their complete conversation. Ilgen told Pipper, "You must crush Medvedev completely. All of our troubles in Rovno come from his atrád. It would be great if you could capture the bandit alive and bring him to this very table."

Pipper answered, "I guarantee that we'll destroy that Medvedev. My troops have never failed — we've always smashed such bandits." Ilgen said, "I've heard about your success — that's why I asked Berlin specially for you. You're reputed to be a genius at this kind of thing! I can supply you with any additional troops that you may need." Pipper answered, "I need no more troops. My division is enough, although I may need some air support." The Ilgen-Pipper conversation took almost two hours. Pipper was given several weeks to study the situation, and then he was to go into action.

Valya told Kuznetsov about this conversation the very next day, and he notified the atrád commanders. They saw a link between Nauminko's disappearance and Pipper's presence. So Lukin sent special agents to find out where Nauminko was working, where he lived, and who his masters were. They soon discovered everything, and Kolya Gnedyuk killed Nauminko in his outhouse. But the damage had already been done — Nauminko had told a great deal to the Germans. They knew our location, our methods of organization and operation, our defensive positions, the means of approach and exit, and so on.

On the anniversary of the October Revolution, we had a party in our atrád — the first such gathering we had had. A group presented a skit, and the festivities lasted until 1 o'clock in the morning. Another atrád commander was invited as a guest; I think it was Saburov, but I'm not sure. I had been back at the atrád for two months since my Rovno spying mission, and I had been reintegrated into the command staff's support group.

Our atrád was protected by three-man outposts located on a ten or twelve kilometer circumference around the atrád encampment. These outposts were two kilometers from each other, and they served as a protective wall. When somebody was sent out of our encampment on a mission, the outposts had to be notified about the number of men involved, their time of departure, and so on. At 4 A.M., after all of the festivities and carousing, we heard shooting from the outposts. General Pipper had exact information about their location, and he was in the process of eliminating them.

Pipper's goal was to smash the atrád completely and finally, and to take Medvedev and the other commanders alive to General Ilgen in Rovno. There were 1,500 men in our atrád, but, as I've said before, at any one time there were usually no more than 800 to 900 in the encampment. When Pipper attacked, 35 percent of our men were absent. Pipper had taken this into account in his planning; he wanted to hit us when we were undermanned and at our weakest.

So, shortly after 4 A.M., an enormous battle started. They had pinpointed our location exactly, although we were hard to get at — the nearest hamlet was nine kilometers away, and the nearest highway was twenty kilometers from our encampment. The battle was a furious one, and the Germans seemed to know exactly where our command staff was located. This was the first occasion when the existence of our whole atrád was threatened — the atrád was fighting for its life.

The Germans had attacked in force. They used planes, 42 mm artillery guns, and heavy mortars. They threw a whole division against us, so we were both outmanned and outgunned. However, their planes weren't of much help to them because we were in a forest. When their commanders fired a red flare to indicate their position, our commanders immediately sent red flares up too, so their bombs landed among them just as often as they landed on us — although we had a fair number of men who were wounded by the shrapnel of the bombs.

I served in a support capacity with our command staff. We never went on fighting engagements; our job was to assist the commanders and keep the staff functioning. We questioned and guarded visitors and prisoners, we controlled access to the commanders, we enforced discipline (e.g. courts-martial), and so on. We served as the commanders' liaison with the atrád; our most trustworthy men carried special instructions to various company commanders. By 10:30 A.M., the noose had tightened. The Germans had moved in to a circumference of two kilometers around the atrád. However, they had pushed so hard towards the command staff that they had created a bulge which brought them only 200 to 300 meters from our commanders.

Our commander in this terrible battle was Commissar Major Sergey Trofimovich Stekhov. By 10:45 A.M., we were almost completely surrounded; the only way in or out was through a 50–60 meter wide muddy marsh. A messenger from another atrád managed to make it through this gap, and he told us that his atrád was only about five kilometers away; his commanders wanted to know if we desired help. I don't know why — to me it seemed that our situation was a very desperate one — but Lukin and Medvedev consulted together and refused the offer of help. They said it was unnecessary. However, at 11 o'clock, all fourteen of us who served our command staff were ordered to leave our duties and take up fighting positions facing the German bulge. The Germans were pushing hard to reach our commanders, and at that time they were only 100 meters from the headquarters hut.

The combat was so intense that at times the fighting was hand-to-hand. I was always coldblooded and practical in battle, but in this fight I lost control of myself. A German was two meters from me, so I leaped on him and bit through his throat. Another German saw what I was doing, so he quickly turned and aimed his submachine gun at me. I was one second, or even less, away from death. Pyotr Mamonyets saw the German wheel around and train his gun on me, so he grabbed his pistol (a captured Mauser) and shot the German. Mamonyets yelled at me, "Kohn, are you crazy? What were you trying to do?" He was right — my leap on the German

[178]

was virtually a suicidal move, and I owe my life to Pyotr Mamonyets.

We were in such desperate straits that by 2 o'clock we were running out of bullets. An order was passed down our lines: those of us who were left were to fire only on individual and specific targets that we could see in our sights. By that time, we were using our guns as clubs and as bayonet-holders.

Victor Semyonov, a company commander (today he's a major in the Moscow Militia), had been called into our commanders' hut at 9 in the morning, and Stekhov had given him an assignment: he was to take a detachment of men and sneak through the marsh, make a detour of seven kilometers, and attack the German division's command post. It was thought that he could reach this objective in two hours; but 4:30 came, and 5:00 too, and we hadn't heard any explosion or unusual sound from the German positions. Time was passing, we were very hard-pressed, and we began to fear the worst — perhaps Semyonov and his men had been annihilated.

It was just starting to get a bit dark when, all of a sudden, we heard a mighty yell of "hoorah" that shook the whole forest. It came from the general direction of the German command post. We picked up the yell and started a charge with our very last bullets. The Germans were seized by a terrific panic — they were sure that they had been surrounded. The hand-to-hand fighting lasted till 8:00. The Germans ran whichever way they could. By 8:30 or 9:00 the last pockets of Germans were cleaned up, and the battle was over.

Semyonov was later asked why it had taken him so long to reach the German command post? He explained that his detachment had been noticed, so he had to eliminate the Germans who had spotted him. He had to be very thorough,

[179]

because one warning from them to their command post would have ruined the whole mission. Also, instead of making a detour of six or seven kilometers, he had to make a much bigger detour and approach the command post from the rear. Semyonov approached the command post, which was 800 meters from the German front lines, so as to eliminate quietly all the guards of the post, and then, like locusts, our men swarmed in and attacked the German staff. The command staff and all its men were destroyed in ten minutes. Victor Semyonov was later promoted to battalion commander as a reward for this successful action. I'm sure that I wouldn't be writing this book now had it not been for Victor Semyonov's great achievement that day in the darkening forest.

Two weeks later we received a German newspaper from Rovno, which said that 250 Germans had been killed in that forest battle and that one of the dead was the famous General Pipper. We didn't take prisoners, but the Germans probably had 750–900 injured in the battle too (3:1 or 4:1 is the usual ratio of injured to killed). The Germans were in such a panic when the tide turned that we were able to capture much valuable military booty. We took 150 special wagons; these were not farmers' wagons, but specially armored wagons built like trucks. The Germans had to use them instead of mechanized vehicles because the area was impassable for cars and trucks. These wagons, pulled by special German draft horses, were full of ammunition. We took nine bazookas too, as well as four 42 mm guns. We took so many machine guns that we didn't know what to do with them.

The fact that General Pipper had received a specific order to destroy Medvedev's atrád was evident from his manner of attacking us. There were other atráds quite near us, but Pipper took a circuitous route to avoid engaging them. He aimed straight for us, and he was appropriately rewarded for his efforts.

When the battle finished, we started to gather our wounded for medical treatment at our field hospital. Just then, we received an urgent order from Moscow to pull out immediately. This order surprised us, because we had won the battle and cleaned the Germans out of our area. All the atráds around us received the same order — to pull out and proceed to western Byelorussia. (I found out later that two days after we pulled out, a massive German attack on our old encampment site took place. The Germans, however, found only a deserted clearing in the forest. Moscow had prior knowledge of this attack, and that is why we received the order to pull out.)

We finished gathering our injured (fifty men) and our dead (eighteen men). However, one of our men was missing. We knew that partisans do not fall alive into the enemy's hands, so we were sure that he must be lying in some thicket, or some bushes. Our atrád waited for two hours; several hundred men were sent to search the area, but they couldn't find the missing partisan, a machine-gunner. This man was a Jew from Rovno — a short fellow, 25 or 26 years old. He had been a cabinetmaker. I don't remember his name, but I know that he hid in an attic when the first slaughter of Rovno Jews took place. He saw the beasts dragging his wife to the slaughter. A year later, we captured the Banderovets who had seized her. I remember how this Rovno cabinetmaker ran over to our company commander and yelled, "I recognize him — he killed my wife! He's a murderer! You must permit me to pay him back!" The Jew's shrieking was terrible — I can hear it to this very day: "You *must* let me! You *must*!" The company commander let our man settle his score with the bloody Banderovets.

The atrád waited for several hours, and then a group was

[181]

left behind to look for the missing man. They didn't find his body until the next morning — he had been killed as a result of a severe head injury. Our atrád was lined up, ready to move off. We had about 100 of our wagons lined up, and about 150 of the captured German wagons. However, we lacked enough men to drive them all. My own commander, Burlotenko, came over to me as I stood in the line and said, "Kohn, take this wagon, harness the horses, and move off." I answered, "Yes, sir, right away," but in my whole life I had never handled horses. I knew a little about riding horseback, but I knew nothing about harnessing horses. And these horses would have to be well harnessed, because we were to proceed down a narrow path; it wasn't even a road.

I took the two lively draft horses and tried to harness them in the rear. I suffered like a dog! I preferred fighting in battle to harnessing those two beasts! I finally succeeded in the rear but in the front — ah, certain chains had to go alongside their mouths with metal bars *in* their mouths, and I was afraid of getting my fingers bitten off. I had no idea how to connect those chains and bars. Meanwhile, night was coming on, and I had to do something. So I took the horses by their heads, and I proceeded on foot, leading them. I walked five or six kilometers like that, until I met that very same Pyotr Mamonyets who had saved my life.

Mamonyets was quite amazed at the sight of me leading the two heavy draft horses through the woods. He said, "Hey, Kohn, why are you leading horses like that? Why don't you sit down on the wagon?" I answered, "I prefer to do it this way." Mamonyets then said, "Who are you fooling? Are you going to lead two horses like this for two hundred kilometers?" I finally got over my shame and told him the truth. I said, "I don't know how even to begin harnessing these horses!"

[182]

At first, Mamonyets didn't say anything. He just nodded his head from side to side, while my face became more and more red. Finally he said, "Kohn, where are you from?" I replied, "I'm from Poland; I lived in Warsaw just before the war." When Mamonyets heard the word "Warsaw" he broke out in a wide grin, went over to my horses, fastened a few connections, adjusted a few straps, and the mighty beasts were harnessed. He said, "*Landsman*, sit down on the wagon with me!" I sat with him on the wagon, and he took the reins and gave me a crash course in horsemanship. He explained, "In Ukrainian, this is *hop*, and that is *hep*. This is right, and that is left. It's so simple." Mamonyets remained with me for a few kilometers until I learned how to handle the horses. And it really was quite simple, once you mastered the basics. In this life, a person must know everything. No type of knowledge, however farfetched it may seem, is useless.

So I drove the horses and wagon all night. When the dawn came, we stopped in a forest for four or five hours. We had to stop because we had several men who had suffered serious head injuries. Those operations that could have been done immediately after the battle were done then; but we also had a number of hopeless, inoperable cases. A bullet in the head often results in an inoperable injury. Medvedev went over to our hospital director, Tsessarsky, who was also his personal friend (they used to play chess together), and asked him, "Perhaps we can try to do something more for these badly injured comrades?" But Tsessarsky answered that nothing more could be done. Medvedev then asked, "How long can these poor fellows last?" Tsessarsky answered that they would be gone in two or three hours. So Medvedev decided, "The atrád will remain here for the next three hours." And so we did — until our last comrade died. We buried our dead in one large grave, and we moved out.

(Shortly after the war, our comrades' bodies were exhumed and moved back to our original encampment site, where Pipper had attacked us. The bodies were reburied together, and a large monument was erected over the grave. Our atrád's encampment was reconstructed to look just as it had been during the war, and a museum was built there explaining Kuznetsov's great achievements. A road from the nearest hamlet — eight or nine kilometers away — was cut through the forest to this reconstructed encampment, and a parking lot and snack bar were built. A hotel was also built in the nearest hamlet. Today, thousands of visitors from the Soviet Union and other countries visit the site of our atrád.)

We were on the move for a whole day and a whole night. The next day we came into western Byelorussia, and we approached a village called Velki-Tselkovichi. It was by now October of 1943. In this area there were Bulbovtsy, not Banderovtsy. These Bulbovtsy (named after their leader, Bulba) were basically the same as the Banderovtsy, but they were not quite as deadly, and they had a smaller organization. They had quite a history of antipartisan combat, because the partisans had organized themselves in western Byelorussia even before they had crystallized in the Ukraine. (The partisans organized in Byelorussia at the end of 1941 and in early 1942, and then they moved into the western Ukraine.) Although we were in Byelorussia for rest and recuperation, we immediately started to clean the Bulbovtsy out of the Velki-Tselkovichi area. We also transferred all our injured, weak, and sick men (approximately 150 people) to Fedorov's atrád. Fedorov's men would transport them closer to the front, in order to place them sooner under the protection of the approaching Red Army.

We remained in Velki-Tselkovichi for about a week. A group of 150 men belonging to our atrád had already been encamped ten or fifteen kilometers past Kolkovich for a year and a half. Their leader was a Captain Brezhnev (no relation to the present Soviet leader). Brezhnev received an order to rejoin us with his men. As soon as they arrived, they lined up, and Captain Brezhnev reported officially to Medvedev. Medvedev greeted the 150 partisans warmly, and then — it was utterly amazing — he snapped an order to our men: Captain Brezhnev was to be placed under arrest immediately. We were quite speechless. We thought that they would embrace, and here Medvedev greeted the ordinary partisans and placed their leader under arrest.

What had happened to warrant such strange behavior? Captain Brezhnev was taken to our command staff immediately, and since I served the staff I knew what was going on. Brezhnev apparently hung back; he was somewhat recalcitrant and avoided engaging the enemy even when he had been ordered expressly to do so. I believe that Medvedev would have had him shot immediately, but Lukin was less harsh and tried to introduce mitigating circumstances as a plea. Brezhnev, who was under detention for over a month, was punished, but his life was spared. He was reduced in rank from a commander to an ordinary partisan.

We went from Velki-Tselkovichi into the dense Byelorussian forest, which began four kilometers from the town. We remained in that forest for several months. Our atrád had been set up mainly to support Kuznetsov in his important work. When we were established at our encampment in the western Ukraine, we were only fifty kilometers from Rovno. When we sent a messenger to Rovno in the morning, he could return the same evening. Now, in Byelorussia, we were 110 kilometers from Rovno, so a messenger making the round trip had to cover a difficult 220 kilometers, which was simply too long. Many times we had to send a whole group on this lengthy trip, because the trip was very dangerous for one person. In effect, then, Kuznetsov no longer was in steady contact with our atrád. When he sent a courier, this courier had to play it by ear — he knew that there were two- or three-man outposts of our atrád scattered here and there, so the courier would try to find the outpost (in Russian it's called a *mayak*), and the outpost would transmit the information to our atrád commanders. The whole process was too chancy, and it took too long.

Our commanders decided, undoubtedly with Moscow's approval, that we had to return to the western Ukraine immediately. Our commanders picked a group of 150 men under the direction of Lukin and Valentin Semyonov; they were to select and prepare a new encampment for us in the western Ukraine. When it was ready, they would notify the rest of our atrád, and we would join them there. So the 150 man detachment moved out, and we remained with Medvedev in the forest near Tselkovichi.

Our group, under Medvedev, often sent small detachments into the neighboring areas (we were eight or ten kilometers from the nearest village that had a mill) to gather intelligence and obtain food, the latter usually being confiscated from known nationalists. In our atrád there were a father and two sons, 17 and 18 years old. Their family name was Primak. One day, early in the morning, these two sons, who had been in the Komsomol together, were sent out as part of one of these small detachments. Later that morning we heard terrific shooting, and we didn't even know its origin — the sounds of the firefight were echoing all over the place. By the time our men found the origin of the shooting, the two Primak brothers had been killed, and several other men had been badly wounded. Our detachment had numbered eight men, and the Bulbovtsy were many, so our men had been surrounded.

The Bulbovtsy lost eight or nine men in this engagement, and we lost the two Primak brothers. It was a heart-rending scene — the corpses of the two brothers, lying there side by side before we buried them. Our men tried to comfort the boys' father, but Primak maintained his self-control and said, "I need no sympathy. My boys gave their lives for a good cause; they tried to spare future generations from the knives and guns of fascist murderers. But . . . but . . . what will I tell my wife? What can I say to her?" And when he said these last two sentences, he started to sob and cry uncontrollably, and threw himself on his sons' bodies. His whole body shook spasmodically as we stood there with the two warm bodies beside the open grave.

Lukin had left with his 150-men detachment and had crossed into the western Ukraine. The Banderovtsy were very well organized at this time. They had become disillusioned with the Germans and with German promises, so they struck out for themselves and organized groups of thosands of men. Lukin's detachment was about a hundred kilometers from us and was making its way, on a narrow path, through a dense forest. Just at that time, in the dead of night, a group of Banderovets officers, who had just finished a three months' crash course at their officers' training school, was moving along the narrow path in the opposite direction. This Banderovets group, numbering about 400 or 500 men, virtually collided with our 150 men in that dense forest. A terrific firefight erupted and lasted about twenty minutes. In those twenty minutes, our 150 men captured 170 rifles, much ammunition, and other supplies. The Banderovtsy had many killed, while Lukin's detachment had only one wounded partisan.

How could our 150 men captu e 170 rifles while suffering almost no losses at all? Such results were not exceptional — they were the norm at that time. The answer can be found in our state of high readiness. We were ready for battle twenty-four hours a day. At the beginning, I had an ordinary rifle. I slept with that rifle, and even when I went to the toilet at night I took my rifle. During the last year of the war, my submachine gun was my constant companion, and we were mentally "on alert" at all times. We expected battle every second of every day, and we knew who and what the enemy was.

Lukin's detachment finally arrived at their destination in the western Ukraine, selected a site for our new encampment, and took several days to prepare it. They radioed back to us that all was ready, so we prepared the atrád and moved back from western Byelorussia into the western Ukraine.

Kuznetsov once managed to kidnap a very highly placed German general who was stationed in Rovno. This was the only case in our atrád's history where a general was captured alive; all of Kuznetsov's other targets were killed in or around their offices. The kidnapped German general was the infamous Ilgen I spoke about earlier; he was responsible for the "disposal" of those people, living in the Ukraine, who had no place in the New Order of the Thousand Year Reich. Ilgen had them killed or shipped out. His official title was: Commander of the Reich's Punitive Troops in the Ukraine. Kuznetsov had wanted permission to kill or kidnap Ilgen, but the atrád, on Moscow's instructions, had refused for eight or nine months to grant such permission. (Our atrád's function was espionage, not assassination.) Moscow did approve the assassination of other key Germans, but Ilgen was, for some strategic reason, left untouched. Finally, when Moscow approved, Ilgen met his end with a special distinction: he was the only German general to be captured alive by partisans. A remarkable woman played a key role in ending Ilgen's nefarious career. Her name was Lydia Lisovskaya.

At the beginning of the occupation, Lydia Lisovskaya worked in a German senior officers' mess. She attempted, from the very beginning, in August and September of 1942, to link up with the partisans, notwithstanding her good job and connections. Russians prisoners of war were brought to her for hard work in the restaurant. She tried to talk those she trusted into escaping to the partisans in the woods. Two of the POWs (one of them was named Volodya Graznikh) agreed to try, and she asked them, if they should be successful, to communicate her address to the partisans. Those two POWs, after some time in the woods, ran into Medvedev's partisans. When they were interrogated, they explained about their supervisor in the restaurant and her encouragement and help. The interrogators couldn't believe them. They said, "She's working at a 'cushy' job for the Germans and yet she instigated your escape? Impossible!" But the POWs insisted, "Yes, and she even gave us food and money for the escape." These remarkable facts were communicated to Lukin and Medvedev. Lukin called Kolya Gnedyuk and sent him to meet that woman and find out exactly what she was up to.

Lydia was under a cloud of suspicion for a long time after the atrád made contact with her. They gave her small, even unnecessary jobs, to test her loyalty. Then Lydia told Kolya Gnedyuk that several colonels, who had just returned from the front, had asked her to set up a party for them at her home. At this party there would also be a major who had just been released from the hospital after a three-months stay. So Gnedyuk asked Lydia, "Do you know Hauptmann Paul Siebert?" "Yes," she said, "I see him in our restaurant from time to time." So Gnedyuk told her, "Invite Siebert to the party too. You might learn something from him." And it was at that party that Lydia and Kuznetsov met for the first time on more than just a casual basis; they were talking together, joking, and enjoying themselves. (That party almost turned into a disaster for Kuznetsov but I'll explain about that near-disaster later.)

After several months, Kuznetsov decided that Lydia Lisovskaya should become General Ilgen's housekeeper, and he asked the atrád commanders for their approval. Lukin insisted that she should be investigated more thoroughly; Kuznetsov had to be 100 percent sure that she was not a double agent. If he could be completely positive about her, then she could be sent to Ilgen, but she was to know nobody from the atrád except Kolya Gnedyuk.

Lydia was put to one final test. Siebert, now dressed in civilian clothes as a secret Gestapo agent, came to visit her. She saw that his hands were covered with blood, and his shirt was also stained. When Lydia asked him about his hands and shirt, Siebert answered; "We were practicing close-range shooting today, so I got splattered with this damn blood. We used new revolvers on Soviet prisoners." Lydia's eyes grew larger with astonishment. She said, "What? You practiced on living people?" Siebert saw the pained look on her face. He saw that she had been emotionally moved. He asked her for water to clean himself and told her to make tea. Then he explained, "I'm serving now as an agent of the plainclothes Gestapo." He took out an employment form from his pocket and asked Lydia to become an agent too. He said, "I'm leaving this form with you. I must go; I'm in a hurry. I'll be by for your answer tomorrow, at eight in the morning. The Reich needs you. Heil Hitler!"

Kuznetsov told Gnedyuk to visit Lydia at 7 A.M. He would see if she mentioned Siebert's terrible offer. When Gnedyuk saw her, she told him everything. She said, "What vermin they are — the worst on earth! All of the time I thought that he was somewhat of a decent German. But don't worry — he won't be around much longer." This last sentence aroused Kolya Gnedyuk's curiosity. He asked her, "What do you have in mind?" Lydia answered, "He'll be here at eight for my answer. I'll poison him. That animal loves tea, so I'll poison his tea. He won't last ten minutes after he drinks my 'special' tea!" Kolya told her, "You mustn't do that now. We can use him to learn things about the Gestapo." However, Lydia was adamant. She said, "I'll obey whatever you order me to do, *except* in this case. The beast must go! You didn't see the blood on his hands and shirt — I did!" Kolya pleaded with her, but to no avail. He saw that Kuznetsov must be warned, so he left Lydia and, with his five men, ran around all of Rovno looking for Kuznetsov. When they finally found him, Gnedyuk told him about his conversation with Lydia; Kolya said, "We must tell her the whole truth. This was a close call — too close for comfort." Kuznetsov agreed, and he told Gnedyuk, "I'll visit her, and you'll come in five minutes later."

So Kuznetsov, alias Paul Siebert, Captain, now serving as a Gestapo agent, went to see Lydia. As he came into her flat, he greeted her with the secret partisan password — "Regards from Popov" — which she had used with Kolya Gnedyuk. When Lydia heard the Gestapo man use the partisan password, she became terribly frightened. She thought the Gestapo had captured Gnedyuk and discovered the truth. Kuznetsov had used the password because he wanted to observe her reactions, and he saw her extreme distress. Just then, Kolya Gnedyuk came in. Kuznetsov gave him the "all-clear" with his eyes, and Kolya told Lydia, "Lydia meet Hauptmann Paul Siebert, *one of our atrád's very best men.*" Well, Lydia's nerves exploded. She burst out crying — the only time anybody ever saw her cry. And this reaction was understandable; Lydia had been tested to the very limits of human endurance.

Kolya and Kuznetsov came to know Lydia very well, and they had faith in this honest woman who had made such efforts to find the partisans. They suggested that she leave the restaurant and go work for General Ilgen. She said that she could easily arrange it, because Ilgen had confided in her and explained his digestive problems to her; he seemed to like her. The Gestapo was also pleased with her. So, in several days, Lydia Lisovskaya was working as a housekeeper for Ilgen, the butcher, and the die was cast.

Kuznetsov picked three men for this unprecedented mission — the kidnapping of a senior German general. Kolya Strutinsky was to serve as a chauffeur, Mietek Stefanski (he lives in Poland today) was to be dressed as a German officer, and Jan Kaminski, also in a German uniform, completed the group.

General Ilgen's residence was located in an area that had been sealed off as exclusively German. Only German colonels and generals could live there, and access to this area was carefully controlled. Ilgen's house was guarded, at all times, by Vlasovites (turncoat Soviet soldiers who had joined the Nazis). The watch at Ilgen's house was rotated every three hours. When Lydia left the front curtain closed, it meant that Ilgen wasn't home. However, when the curtain was open a bit, it meant that Ilgen was home.

On the appointed day, Lydia was a bit over-anxious. She left the curtain open because she expected Ilgen at any moment; however, when our four men moved in on the house, Ilgen was not yet at home. The Vlasovite guard at the door stopped them, but Kuznetsov had a special pass issued by the highest authorities, allowing him to go everywhere. The guard, after examining the pass, told them to come in;

he ordered Kolya Strutinsky to take off his gun and put it aside. Kolya pretended to obey, while Kuznetsov pointed his own revolver at the guard and said, "Drop your rifle. If you obey, you'll live!" The guard saw how he had been duped, so he dropped the rifle. Kuznetsov took the bullets out of the guard's rifle, gave it back to him, and put him back at his guard booth. Kolya Strutinsky was on the other side of the booth, posing as a guard and keeping an eye on the Vlasovite. The idea was that the general should see at his door the man he was used to seeing there. The guard was changed every three hours, and "our" guard had been standing there for two hours already, so we had only another hour to complete the job.

In a short time, General Ilgen came home. While he was taking off his coat, Kuznetsov approached him. The General asked, at first somewhat naively, "How did you get in here?" Then he started to shout. Kuznetsov answered, "Don't yell! I've been sent to arrest you. I have my orders!" The General saw that something was wrong with the whole business, and he tried to escape. A major scuffle followed. Kuznetsov was strong, but Ilgen was young and a former athlete. He was on the point of breaking loose when Kolya came in. He hit Ilgen on the head, and then they bound and gagged him. All this was supposed to take place in ten minutes, but it took longer. They had very little time left to get out of there.

They dragged the General out of the house towards the car, but as they were doing this, Ilgen managed to spit out the gag in his mouth. He started to bellow, "*Hilfe! Hilfe!*" (Help! Help!) Just at that time, two German officers were walking by. One was Koch's chauffeur, and the other was a liaison man with the front. The liaison man was on his way to the train station, and the other officer was accompanying him. They heard the yelling, the cries for help, so they came running and asked what was going on. Kuznetsov, who had rapidly gagged Ilgen again and placed a sack on his head, answered, "We caught a Soviet spy dressed as a general of the Reich. We have to take him to the military police station." The two German officers insisted on going to the station too. They saw how this enemy agent tried to resist. They had even helped to subdue him, hadn't they? They wanted to gain credit for assisting in the capture of a dangerous spy. They *had* to go to the station too. Kuznetsov first asked to see their papers, and examined them carefully. Then he was quick to agree with them; they were, after all, "valuable witnesses." However, he told them that he needed only one of them, the chauffeur. The liaison officer could go. The car was a small one, so they were all stuffed into it like sardines. Even with that stuffing, there was no room for fat Jan Kaminski (who had been a baker in Poland before the war). So Kolya shoved Jan into the trunk, and they drove off.

They drove for a while, and then they passed the Ukrainian police station. A few minutes later they passed the military police station. Koch's chauffeur said, "Here it is — here's the military police station. Stop!" Kuznetsov answered, "No, no — we have a special counter-intelligence station. This is not a Gestapo matter or an ordinary military police arrest. It is quite special." They drove on, and the chauffeur saw that they were leaving the city. He knew that something was wrong, and he wanted to start yelling, so he was also gagged. (His weapon had been taken from him earlier.) The car proceeded to a house ten kilometers outside of Rovno occupied by a Polish agent of our atrád, Valentin Teichmann. The house was located near Novidvor. Vale Burin had used Teichmann's house three or four times before to repaint Kuznetsov's car to disguise it. (Burin's own house was the second safehouse used by our atrád in Rovno; Ivan Prikhodko's was the first.) Koch's chauffeur was killed immediately, but Ilgen was interrogated at length. He refused to talk, and he required some "encouragement"; he finally told our people quite a bit.

Ilgen had to be killed in that house. By sheer coincidence, great numbers of German soldiers were passing through the area, and a large group of them decided to camp in the courtyard of the very building where our men were questioning Ilgen. When Ilgen heard their voices, he clammed up and refused to say another word. He felt that his rescuers were near. So, after six hours of interrogation, Ilgen was killed. He was buried in the shed, and all of his documents were brought back to the atrád's encampment.

Lydia Lisovskaya was a beautiful human being, both physically and spiritually. She used to wear a gold crucifix, and she went to church every day. A long time after the Ilgen episode, Lydia retreated with the Germans to Lvov (Lemberg), as she had been ordered to do by our atrád. When the Red Army took Lvov, she reported to the Red Army authorities and explained who she was. After two weeks, she was notified that she was needed in Rovno. A truck was sent for her, but the truck kept going and it passed Rovno. Some fifty kilometers, perhaps more, out of Rovno, Lydia Lisovskaya was killed. It pains me even today to think about it. It seems that German counterintelligence knew about her accomplishments and wanted to settle the score with her, so she met her end two weeks after Lvov was taken.

I promised to say more about that party Lydia organized for German officers, when she got to know Kuznetsov. Many months before that party, Kuznetsov had been told to return from Rovno to our encampment and report to the commanders. Our commanders explained that many very high-ranking German generals had made special trips to the Vinnitsa area. All of those generals had the same destination, but they traveled in great secrecy, and no Soviet agent could even come close to penetrating their Vinnitsa destination. Our commanders wanted to capture a high-ranking German officer for detailed interrogation. They needed this information immediately, so there was a certain urgency about the whole matter.

Lukin worked out a plan. Our men would not resort to our usual ambush tactic of digging in beside a road or hiding behind trees. They would stage an open ambush. Our men would travel openly, on the road, in wagons, and they would kidnap a high officer. Kuznetsov was told that he would lead this kidnapping expedition.

The plan was elaborated in the following way. Our first man on the road would be Kolya Gnedyuk, dressed as a Ukrainian farmer, carrying a basket of apples and eggs. He would examine the German military cars going by him from the opposite direction. These cars were moving fast, but Kolya would have a chance to notice their occupants. He would ignore low-ranking German officers, but when he saw a senior officer he would fire a flare. Farther down the road Kuznetsov, dressed as a German officer, would be driving a wagon. He would be accompanied by four of our men, dressed as Ukrainian policemen. Still farther on, 150 meters away, would be another wagon with five more of our men, also dressed as Ukrainian policemen.

They set out on the road, which was the main Lutsk-Rovno highway. Many vehicles coming from Kiev used this road. Kolya Gnedyuk let about ten cars pass, and then he saw several senior officers sitting in a passing car. He fired his flare, but the driver heard a shot and accelerated rapidly. The car passed Kuznetsov's wagon; Kuznetsov tried to immobilize the car by hitting its tires with submachine gun bullets, but the car somehow remained untouched. The car still had to pass our other wagon, and one of the five men on that wagon was George Strutinsky, who was a crack shot. The car was already 300 meters past him, but he used his submachine gun to fire at its tires, and he succeeded. The driver lost control, the car skidded erratically toward a thicket at the side of the road, and finally it turned over.

As soon as the car turned over, our men ran over to it and pulled out the officers. Several were already dead, but some were alive. The highest-ranking officer, a Colonel Reiss, was the head of military communications for the whole front. He was very highly placed, and his capture resulted in extremely important discoveries.

Kuznetsov led the team that interrogated Reiss for several days. From Reiss the Soviet authorities learned that Hitler had a complete military general staff operating in a forest near Vinnitsa. It was near a village named Yakushintsy. An elaborate command center had been built completely underground, and with all its support facilities, it was almost a subterranean village. Whole forests had been planted on it to mask it from observation. From Berlin to Vinnitsa, a trench that was one and a half meters deep had been dug. This communications trench, which assured a direct Berlin-Vinnitsa link, was built over a period of many months by 20,000 Soviet prisoners. Kuznetsov asked Colonel Reiss, "Where are those 20,000 prisoners-of-war?" Reiss answered coldly, "Where the enemies of the Reich belong — in their graves! We 'disposed' of them — they knew too much." He spoke of 20,000 lives as a normal person would speak of disposing of old banana peels. His coldness and his inhumanity were unbelievable.

At first, our interrogators thought that the communications trench was used by Hitler to send orders from Berlin to the Ukraine. They soon learned that, during certain periods, Hitler himself had directed the war *from Vinnitsa*. Goering had a whole installation that he personally used in this command bunker. So the commands often went from Vinnitsa to Berlin, and not vice versa. All of our information was speedily transmitted to Moscow, and they apparently tapped that Berlin-Vinnitsa communication line for a lengthy period of time. They learned much from it of enormous military significance until the Germans uncovered the tap.

During the open ambush that resulted in the capture of Reiss, Kuznetsov found a very modern nickel-plated revolver beside the overturned car. This revolver was of a new type nobody had seen before. Kuznetsov brought the revolver back to the command staff in our atrád, and our leaders suggested that he leave the revolver in the atrád. Kuznetsov, however, asked for permission to keep it, and he was granted this permission.

When Lydia made that party for German officers, she invited Kuznetsov too. The fifteen officers who came had a great time; they ate and drank, and then drank some more. When they were all quite tipsy, each officer took his revolver out, put it on the table, and gave a short speech describing how he had obtained his pistol and what it had accomplished — how many Jews it had finished off, how many Gypsies it had "taken care" of, and the like. As each exploit was recounted, the fellow officers cheered, pounded the table, and jumped up in joy.

Kuznetsov's turn came, and he saw that there was no way out for him — he had to fabricate a story. So he took out his revolver and put it down on the table. As soon as he did this, a German major, named Wiener, exclaimed, "My God, that's my revolver!" This Major Wiener was an engineering expert involved in the testing of new weapons; he had been Colonel Reiss's assistant. He told the officers at the party all about his close call many months before when his car was ambushed on the open road during a trip back to Rovno from Kiev. He had jumped from the car and, although injured, had managed to escape by sheer luck. He explained how Colonel Reiss, his fellow passenger, had disappeared, and how Graf von Daam, a senior communications advisor, had been killed in the ambush. It seems that our men had not noticed that one German had escaped during the ambush.

Major Wiener asked, "What's the serial number on that revolver?" Kuznetsov kept his control; his calculated self-control was his big asset. The serial number had six or seven digits, so when he read the number out he changed one of the digits. The Major said, "Read it again, Hauptmann! You're sure you're reading correctly?" Kuznetsov answered, "Of course I'm sure! Look for yourself!" The Major glanced in a perfunctory way at the revolver, but he was too drunk to concentrate, and the others were quite drunk too. He said, "Ah, yes, I lost such a revolver when the bandits ambushed us. What a revolver it was. . . . You could hit a dirty Jew half a kilometer away with it. I once tested it on a Gypsy. . . ." And he launched himself on a lengthy discourse about his glorious past and soon forgot about the revolver.

This was a close call for Kuznetsov. There was a Gestapo officer, Major Kondrack, at the party too, and he said little, but he had observed the whole scene. He did not drink quite as much as the others. Kondrack was Kuznetsov's "friend," but his suspicions were growing. Kondrack, however, wasn't sure, so he didn't share his suspicions with anybody. He kept his ideas to himself, "for further investigation." He later told Valya Dovger that there was something "fishy" about Hauptmann Siebert — that Kuznetsov was possibly a British plant in the German ranks. Valya told Kuznetsov, and they seized the Major during a dinner at Valya's house. Strutinsky and Kuznetsov bound his hands and feet and gagged him. Kuznetsov then told him that his suspicions were right — his "friend" and brother officer was a spy; however, he was a Soviet spy, and not an Englishman. Major Kondrack was then repaid for his glorious Gestapo career. Our men concealed his body in a sack, and they soon got rid of that sack and its rotten contents.

In the early fall of 1943, Kuznetsov struck up a friendship with a German officer, Otto von Ortel. Kuznetsov tried to figure out who this von Ortel was but was unsuccessful. When he reported to our atrád commanders, he told them, "I've met many German officers, and I could usually size them up, figure them out. But this von Ortel is absolutely a mystery to me. He has a very secretive air about him; he keeps to himself. He's a brilliant intellectual; he knows literature very well, and he has a very advanced musical knowledge."

Once, when Kuznetsov was with Ortel in an officers' mess, Ortel called a Russian dishwasher over to the table and spoke to him in perfect, idiomatic Russian. Kuznetsov wondered: how could SS Sturmbannführer Ortel speak perfectly fluent Russian? Kuznetsov asked him, "Where did you learn to speak Russian?" Ortel answered, "Ah, dear Siebert, I've been interested in that for a very long time. Do you understand Russian, Siebert?" Kuznetsov answered, "Two or three words — like every officer serving on this front. You pick up a word here and a word there." Ortel laughed, "I spoke with many Russians on various subjects and on no occasion did they figure out that I'm not a Russian. Before the war I lived in Moscow for two years." Kuznetsov asked, "And what did you do there?" Ortel answered, "Things, dear Siebert, many things. . . ." Kuznetsov smiled, "Ah, so you were a spy." Ortel replied, "You could call it spying, but I would call it serving the Führer and the Fatherland." Kuznetsov, with a laugh, said, "Let's not talk about this any more. We military men don't particularly like that kind of work — cloak and dagger stuff. We don't really care for it." Ortel answered, "I can tell you one thing: I did more damage to the rotten Bolshies than your whole regiment."

Kuznetsov communicated this conversation to the atrád commanders, and it was retransmitted to Moscow. After several days, Kuznetsov again met Ortel, who told him, "Siebert, I can tell you that our high leaders are not as idealistic as they used to be. They're out for their own power and reputations now!" Kuznetsov didn't answer; he just thought for a little while. Ortel noticed that he hadn't replied, so he said, "Siebert, you don't have to fear me. I wear our uniform with pride. Better be afraid of those who masquerade in civilian clothes. I myself am afraid of them. Do you know Major Martin Gettel?" Kuznetsov answered, "I've seen him around. I know that he works at the Gebietskommissariat." Ortel said, "Paul, I'm telling you something; I'm your friend. Your fiancée, Valya Dovger, should be very, very careful with him!"

Once, Gettel had told Valya that he wanted to walk her home after work (they worked in the same building). Valya couldn't refuse him. Gettel asked, "Look how there's no justice in the world! I've been in Rovno so long, and I haven't met one decent girl. Paul Siebert comes from the front, and here he finds such a beauty! But I can tell you that you have caught my eye, Valya, and I know a good woman when I see one. Tell me, have you known Siebert for a long time?" She answered, "Not such a long time." He said, "Tell me about the first time you met him. I want to know all about it." They

[201]

arrived at Valya's place, and Gettel said to her, "I hope to accompany you home many times in the future."

The contents of this conversation were immediately communicated to Kuznetsov, and Valya told him that at work nobody knew what Gettel did, what his function was. Although he worked in the Gebietskommissariat, he was in no way connected with the work that went on there. Even the cleaning women who cleaned the offices in the early morning had no right to enter Gettel's office. He cleaned his own place. He lived alone. No acquaintances came to see him, nor did he go with anybody. Kuznetsov told Medvedev and Lukin exactly what Valya had told him.

Our commanders started to think that perhaps the Germans were already on the trail of Kuznetsov. They thought about it for a time, and they decided that Kuznetsov should remain in Rovno and that he should be very careful with Gettel. If he should smell in any way that Gettel had discovered that he was not a German, then Gettel was to be eliminated. Our commanders intensified the security arrangements around Kuznetsov in Rovno, the number of people who watched over him was augmented, and his protection was intensified.

Kuznetsov returned to Rovno, and the first to greet him was Maya, Lydia Lisovskaya's cousin. She gave him a message that Ortel wanted to see him. Kuznetsov met Ortel and Maya that evening. Ortel said, "Siebert, I'm repeating my earlier advice to you. Your fiancée should stay very, very far from Gettel!" Kuznetsov laughed, "What — is Gettel such a pining, anguished, moonstruck lover?" Ortel said, "I'm telling you — I met this Gettel at Himmler's Command Headquarters in Berlin — Number Eight, Prinz Albertstrasse. Only the deadliest types move in that milieu." Just then Maya came in, so they started to laugh and kid around, and they changed the subject.

At that time, Gettel went to see Lydia Lisovskaya and told her, "The fact that I've come to see you and what we are to discuss is top secret; nobody must know about it. And I'm underlining this to you again: *absolutely nobody must know about this!* Do you know Hauptmann Paul Siebert?" She said, "Yes." He continued, "How long have you known him? Where did you meet him?" She said, "You know that after work many officers come to my place. I have a phonograph; we have good food and the best drinks." Gettel was all ears; he said, "You never noticed any English words used by Siebert?" Lydia said, "I don't understand or speak English at all. I probably wouldn't recognize an English word if I heard one." "Okay," Gettel said, "when you see Siebert again, be very nice to him, but listen carefully to his speech. Look out for the word 'Sir.' The English like to use that word. You listen for it! And if you hear him say it, let me know immediately — even in the middle of the night!"

Kuznetsov learned about Lydia's conversation with Gettel. But Lydia added, "He didn't ask any pointed questions about the fact that I know you; he just thinks that you're another officer to me. So we can rest easy on that account."

At the end of October 1943, Kuznetsov met Gettel at Lydia's house. The table was covered with food and drink; Kuznetsov took off his revolver and ammunition belt and hung them up on a hook in the closet. He suggested that Gettel do the same — they should all feel at ease. Gettel hesitated; then he too hung his revolver and ammunition belt on a wall hook. They drank to the Führer, discussed the military situation, and Gettel suggested that they drink a toast to that beauty, Valya Dovger. They drank that toast with much enthusiasm and warmth.

Just then, an ordinary German private came in and sat down at the table with the officers. Gettel saw this, so he jumped up and started to yell, "What right do you have to sit at an officers' table? You're only a lousy Pole!" Although Kolya Strutinsky went around as a Volksdeutscher, the Germans still regarded him as half Polish. Kuznetsov also jumped up and started to scold the soldier. At that moment, when Kuznetsov stood up, he went behind Gettel's chair and pinned his hands to his side, while Strutinsky jumped up, took a rope from his pocket, and bound Gettel's hands. (Kuznetsov, after the Kondrack incident, knew exactly how to proceed in such cases.)

Gettel couldn't figure out what was going on. Kuznetsov told him, "Be quiet; nothing can help you now! If you'll cooperate, I'll make things easier for you. I can tell you that I am a spy, but not an English spy as you thought. I'm a Soviet agent." (Gettel had made the same mistake Major Kondrack had made earlier — mistaking Kuznetsov for an English spy.) When Gettel heard this, he exclaimed, "Impossible!"

Kuznetsov interrogated him for over an hour. He found out everything about him — Gettel was a senior counterintelligence man who operated outside the regular channels. Gettel still wouldn't believe that Kuznetsov was a Soviet spy. The questioning ended, and Kuznetsov asked him, "Why did you think all of this time that I was an Englishman?" Gettel answered, "I couldn't imagine such a talented and refined person among the Soviets; you know German literature so well, and you know the geography of Germany better than I know it. I was sure that you were sent by the British Secret Service." Kuznetsov found out that Gettel had kept his suspicions to himself — he wanted to follow them up on his own in order to get sole credit for uncovering a deadly and dangerous enemy agent. Kuznetsov said, "Now, tell me whatever you know about Otto von Ortel." Gettel said, "I can't tell you anything about him because he's a mystery to me. I know everything about everybody, but he remains a riddle to me." Kuznetsov didn't believe him, and he pressured Gettel, who said, "I can tell you only that I once met him in Berlin, at Number Eight Prinz Albertstrasse. Here in Rovno he never went into the Gestapo quarters, but practically everyday he went into a building that housed dentists' offices. He used to spend several hours there every day. I know nothing more about him. He was probably working in that dentists' place under some kind of cover." Gettel was finished off after that interrogation.

When Kuznetsov next met Ortel, the latter said, "Siebert, I've told you before and I'm telling you again: I find that you're a very nice fellow. I have respect for you, and I respect very few people. Tell me, do you have three or four friends who would get along very well with us?" Ortel smiled, "You're an odd guy! You were injured twice by the Russians, and you were decorated twice, yet you're still trying to get back to the front." Kuznetsov stood up as if he were unhappy with Ortel's talk. "Herr Sturmbannführer," he said, "my duty is to fight for the Führer and our Fatherland." Ortel said, "Very good, Siebert, very good! But why do you have to get so upset and official with me? I'm not your commanding officer. Besides, why do you figure that the battlefield is the only place to fight the enemy?" Ortel stopped and thought, and then he continued, "What would you say if I were to suggest to you that you change your function and serve as a spy?" Kuznetsov started to laugh, "What, me a spy? I'm a born infantry man. You are going to turn an infantry man into a spy? I'd never be good at that sort of thing. I can tell you that from the first time I heard about your occupation, I didn't like it at all." Ortel was not to be put off. He went on, "Paul, when you drink beer for the first time it is also not very pleasant. But you acquire a taste for it. Let me be the judge as to whether you'll make a good spy." With that remark the conversation ended.

That conversation was reported to our commanders, who

sent the report on to Moscow. Lukin spoke to Kuznetsov, "When you go back to Rovno, meet him again. Continue to play the game, but don't commit yourself. Try to find out exactly what he's trying to draw you into. Everything is possible. Remember — he could be a provocateur. You have to be very, very careful."

Kuznetsov returned to Rovno. The first one he met was the young and beautiful Maya. Ortel was in love with her, and he trusted her. She found out many things from him and told them to Kuznetsov. When Maya met Kuznetsov, she said, "My German chief at work plans to travel with Ortel very, very far, on an extremely important mission. He told me that he's been given a very vital assignment." Kuznetsov asked, "Where's he going?" Maya's chief, however, hadn't told her about his destination. Kuznetsov said, "Maya, you have to try to follow this up, to find out exactly where they're going. It's very important; something is brewing." Maya said, "He didn't tell me anything else. Oh, yes, I almost forgot; he told me that when he comes back he's going to bring me the finest Persian tapestries to beautify my flat." Kuznetsov said, "Let him feel that you're very close to him; let him confide everything to you. Every word may be of prime importance."

Kuznetsov met Ortel in the officers' mess the next morning. Ortel was in very good spirits. He told Kuznetsov, "Siebert, I'm soon going to introduce you to my best associate, Sturmbannführer Otto Skorzeny." Kuznetsov said, "But Ortel, you still haven't told me what my function will be, what I will be doing." "I'll tell you everything when the time comes," Ortel said. "Skorzeny is the secret SS Chief of Special Missions. Siebert, you're my friend. I can tell you that after Stalingrad and especially after Kursk, our military situation has degenerated very rapidly. It's extremely precarious; only a miracle can help us now. It's possible that Skorzeny and I can create this miracle. Our leaders have given us a very, very special mission: we have to get into Iran. The three Allied leaders — Churchill, Roosevelt, and Stalin — will meet there. I and my group, and Skorzeny and his group, have to liquidate those three Allied leaders. That will provide the miracle we need."

When Kuznetsov heard that, it was as if his feet had been knocked out from under him. This was of stupendous importance! Ortel told Kuznetsov, "Our departure will take place in a number of small groups so as not to attract attention. Our people are being specially trained in a commando assassination school in Copenhagen. You, Paul, will travel there where you'll be trained." Kuznetsov replied, "If you have such confidence in me, then I'm ready to go!" And that's how their conversation ended.

That evening, Kuznetsov returned to our atrád. Our commanders perceived that he was a bit overwrought, which was extremely rare for Kuznetsov. When Kuznetsov had told everything, Medvedev said, "Perhaps you can get me a photo of Ortel?" Kuznetsov answered, "It's impossible. First of all, he avoids people — he doesn't socialize. Second, he wears his cap visor low on his face, so that you can't see his complete face as he walks down the street." Medvedev and Lukin thought it over, and Medvedev suggested, "Try to sketch him. Here's a piece of paper. Write down his dominant characteristics — his height, hair color, weight, and so on. Try something." Kuznetsov worked for an hour and a half on this. All of the information was radioed to Moscow that very same evening.

Kuznetsov never met Ortel again. When he came to Rovno, he went to Maya's place at 15 Legionov Street, and she told him that the SS had called her in and told her that Sturmbannführer von Ortel had committed suicide by shooting himself. That's what they told her, but she never saw the dead body.

At the end of November 1943, Roosevelt learned that the Germans had parachuted several commando groups into Iran. Stalin had, however, established extraordinary security measures, and he suggested that Roosevelt move into the Soviet Embassy compound, a suggestion Roosevelt accepted. The British Embassy wasn't far from the Soviet one, so the Soviet security screen covered the British too. The parachuted Germans were eliminated one after another.

In November of 1943, Kuznetsov had another close call, when he assassinated one of the bloodiest monsters in occupied Eastern Europe, General Alfred Funk, the Chief Judge of the Ukraine. Alfred Funk was a mass murderer. Every day he signed the death warrants of hundreds, or even thousands, of innocent people. A number of plans to kill him were examined in the atrád. They thought of kidnapping him from his residence; he would be more approachable than some other generals, for example those involved in intelligence work or strategic planning. But they decided that, because all the death sentences emanated from Funk's building on Skolna Street, he should be punished there, where he signed away the lives of so many innocent people.

Medvedev, Lukin, and Kuznetsov investigated the matter very carefully, and they found out that Funk went for a shave at 8:30 every morning. At 9 he started to work. Five minutes before 9 he would leave the barbershop and go right into his building, which was only 150 meters away. He had to cross a street, today called Lenina, and there was Skolna Street, on which the three-storey justice ministry building was located. All of the other employees had to be at their desks at twenty minutes before 9, so that when the great man himself, Funk, came in, everybody was at his place, and the wheels of "justice" were rolling smoothly.

Kuznetsov first studied the justice ministry building thoroughly — all the back doors, windows, side entrances, staircases, the number of stairs on each of them, what door Funk used to enter the building, his office on the second floor, and all the rest. Everything was thoroughly analyzed. Jan Anchak, a former captain in the Polish Army, was working in Rovno as a barber. Jan Kaminski was also a Pole, and those two played a key role in this operation. The car driver was Kolya Strutinsky, and the execution itself was done by Kuznetsov.

The plan was as follows: three or four minutes before Funk was to leave the barbershop, Jan Anchak, the barber, was to open the front curtain of the shop a little bit. Kaminski would stand outside the barbershop, six or seven meters away, and when he saw that the curtain had been opened, he would start to scratch the back of his head. This would mean that the murderer would soon come out. When the curtain was completely opened, it meant that Funk was coming out immediately. Then Kaminski was to take off his hat completely. Kuznetsov was to observe these signals.

For weeks, Kuznetsov had been studying and observing Funk's face. Kuznetsov went up to the third floor of the ministry building, and all went as planned. Through a window in the building he saw all of Kaminski's signals. Kuznetsov had planned to accost Funk halfway between the first and second floors, but he had made a slight miscalculation, and he was too early by thirty seconds. So Kuznetsov went into the shadow of a pillar to let the half a minute pass. He saw the shadow of an approaching figure, ascertained that it was the deadly Funk, went over to him, and pumped him full of bullets from his silencer-equipped pistol.

Kuznetsov went out to the waiting car, which sped off towards Zamkova Street. By coincidence, a big truck full of

SS men was parked there, but Kolya Strutinsky managed to drive past the truck before the hue-and-cry started. Jan Kaminski had remained behind to observe the Germans' reactions to Funk's murder: how the alarm was given, and so forth. Well, the alarm was certainly given. Kuznetsov's car had just passed the SS truck when a panic started. The windows of the ministry building were flung open, and people started to yell that Funk had been killed. The city was sealed, and a dragnet operation started. Kuznetsov alone had little chance of getting out of Rovno; only Kolya Strutinsky might bring it off. Every few hundred yards there were military police checkpoints, where all identification papers and special permits and authorizations were carefully scrutinized. The word had gone out: a bandit in German uniform had killed the "precious" Funk. Strutinsky, as usual, served as the driver, while Kuznetsov, in his Hauptmann Paul Siebert disguise, sat in the back.

Kuznetsov saw that it was utterly impossible for him to get out of Rovno. Somebody at one of those checkpoints might get lucky, and that would mean the end of Kuznetsov and Strutinsky and their important activities. Kuznetsov made a decision. If they couldn't go anywhere, they might as well become part of the operation to catch Funk's assassin.

Kuznetsov ordered Kolya to drive to the next corner, and to park the car at a certain angle. He then created his own checkpoint. Kuznetsov stood in the middle of the road, stopped cars, and checked papers. He questioned both drivers and passengers carefully. After two hours, the Gestapo drove by with their truck-mounted loudspeaker and told all Germans that the checkpoints could be disbanded; the operation was over. Kolya then drove the car to a safe-house three or four kilometers outside of Rovno.

The Germans were not, however, sleeping. They had already established the fact that all of the Rovno assassinations were the work of one man: a spy masquerading as a German officer. For some unknown reason, they subscribed to the theory that the spy was an Englishman, not a Russian, but they were on the alert now. Valya Dovger had already been caught in Rovno, and several groups had been arrested too. They were to have retreated, but they were picked up before they could move out. The noose was tightening around Kuznetsov's neck.

By this time, the Germans were retreating across a broad front in the east. When the Germans retreated from Zhitomir, which was about 150 kilometers from Rovno, a terrific panic gripped the Germans in Rovno. Zhitomir had been defended with fanatical determination by diehard SS troops. The fighting was of the hand-to-hand, street-to-street, room-to-room variety. Hardly a building was left standing, and yet the Red Army rolled over the "supermen." The front was approaching Rovno, and chaos ensued. Our atrád commanders were insistent on one point: the Rovno railroad station had to be blown up, no matter what.

The mission was entrusted to Misha Shevchuk and Borisov. Shevchuk was the head of this operation. The explosives were packed into two large valises, along with the time detonators.

However, approaching the railroad station was impossible — absolutely impossible. The Germans, taught by dire necessity, had learned the hard way how to organize a retreat. There were ten checkpoints on all the approaches to the station. You had to have a special evacuation pass, a permit, to get past those checkpoints, and they weren't available to ordinary soldiers. Only senior officers could get such passes enabling them to be evacuated towards Lvov, towards the West. Misha, using a carriage pulled by several horses, made many attempts, but he couldn't get near the station. He would get past a number of checkpoints, but then he would be turned back.

Misha's strongest asset was his inventiveness; he was always capable of improvising, getting around obstacles. Once he saw a German colonel dragging two packed valises in the street. The colonel was covered with sweat — he was breathing hard as he tugged his two valises. Misha ordered Borisov to turn the carriage towards the colonel. The chaos and panic in Rovno was so great that many carriages and cars passed half or three-quarters empty; the supermen were out to save only their own skins, and the occupants of those vehicles had a devil-take-the-hindmost attitude. Misha and Borisov drove over to the colonel, who asked them where they were going? "To the train station," Misha said, and the colonel begged, "Please, take me with you." Misha said, "Yes, sir." He was deferential and respectful, as was only proper when addressing an officer of the Reich. Misha grabbed the colonel's valises and hoisted them on board the carriage, sat the colonel down, and calmed him.

They traveled together — through one checkpoint, another checkpoint, and another. The colonel kept showing his special pass, and it worked wonders. When they came close to the station, they found a company of SS troops surrounding the station, controlling the entrance gates. The SS men didn't want to let them all into the station, but the colonel said, "Let them pass — they're with me." They came into the main hall of the station, and there was no room to sit down — people were packed together like sardines. Everybody was gripped by panic, and the evacuation trains came very sporadically because the rails had been blown up in many places. Misha, Borisov, and the colonel went into a room reserved for senior officers. Misha found a bit of free floor space there, sat the colonel down, put the valises near him (adding to his two valises a third one, full of explosives), and told him, "Look, my friend and I must push our way through to the ticket windows. Our tickets weren't correctly punched when they were issued to us. We'll be back soon. Do you want us to bring you a snack now?" The colonel said, "No, I'll wait till you return, and then we'll all eat together." Misha and Borisov made their way out of that officers' room, pushed their way through the crowded station hall, and left the station. It was now evening.

The timer kept ticking away, and a short time later a tremendous, earth-shaking explosion rocked the Rovno railroad station. The walls collapsed. An enormous panic ensued. A German troop train passing through heard that terrific explosion. They started to yell that the Soviets had parachuted a commando squad there, so the explosion survivors were seized with even greater panic, and they started shooting. The SS troops surrounding the station, hearing the shooting, started to fire back into the ruined building. The troops in the troop train, seeing that they were being fired upon, joined in the shooting. A bitter firefight started, and it went on for ten minutes before peace could be restored. The Germans suffered very heavy casualties in the explosion, especially among their officers.

Today, one of the most modern railroad stations in the Soviet Union has been built on that spot, and there is an imposing plaque on the wall. It says that Kuznetsov used to work there, and that on this-and-this date the railroad hall was blown up by two men from Medvedev's atrád, Shevchuk and Borisov.

We had been told that we would link up with the Red Army when it entered Rovno; our partisan war would be over then. At the beginning of 1944, however, we received

[213]

an order from Moscow: Medvedev's partisans were to fall back to Galicia with the Germans. We were to retreat with the beasts, and we were not supposed to wait for the arrival of the Red Army. Frankly, we were all distressed by this order. I had had enough, and most of our men felt the same way. We didn't express our feelings openly, but we could feel in each other the same thought — that we had done our share. However, an order is an order: we were to retreat with the Germans from Rovno to Lvov.

First, a group of forty of our men was sent to Lvov to prepare an encampment for us; this was to serve as Kuznetsov's base and would enable him to continue his work. The encampment site was supposed to be forty kilometers from Lvov. Boris Krutikov (today a lecturer in Lvov) was the leader of this preparatory group, but he was unable to do much because he lost over eighty percent of his group. We soon found out why he took such a beating.

When we followed some time later we found the going very, very difficult. The Germans used the main roads, so we used the back roads and forest trails. But at times we had no choice — we had to go up onto the main roads too. Our progress was painfully slow, because for a distance of 240 kilometers we had to battle our way through *every* village and hamlet. The Germans weren't a problem — they were busy retreating. Our problems was the Banderovtsy; they were fanatically against the entry of the Soviets. They could see the handwriting on the wall — the Germans were obviously on the run — and so these Ukrainian nationalists contested every meter of land in frantic desperation. We had to battle our way through. These engagements would take half an hour or perhaps an hour; I would estimate that at least 60 percent of the population of these villages and hamlets collaborated actively with the Germans. We were almost 1,500 men, and we found the going very, very hard, so you can imagine what happened to Krutikov's tiny group when they ran into the same fanatical resistance; they were almost massacred, and they couldn't accomplish very much.

We had already reached Lutsk, and from there we were to move in the direction of Lvov. Just at the beginning of sunrise one day, in a village on the outskirts of Lutsk, I was called into the commanders, and Lukin told me, "Kohn, take these two valises. Go to the road; an Opel car will be waiting on the soft shoulder. Kuznetsov will be in that car. Give him these valises." We had just arrived at that village ten hours before, and I didn't know that area, just past Lutsk, at all. I felt a bit nervous.

I had thought that those two valises would be light, but they were very heavy. I could hardly pick them up. I took them and walked slowly to a hill. There was a dirt track going down this hill and leading to a highway at the bottom. I walked 150 meters down this track and I came to the highway, where I saw a waiting Opel car, parked on the shoulder with its motor idling. I recognized Kuznetsov. Belov, a member of our atrád whom I knew well, was now serving as his chauffeur. Looking through the rear window of the car, I could see a man in civilian clothes sitting in the back. He was quite stout and wore a prewar type Polish hat.

I asked Kuznetsov where to put the valises? He said, "Open the rear door and put them in." Then he dismissed me, and the car started to move off. I went back twenty meters and turned around. From afar I saw that there were columns of retreating German troops, and Kuznetsov had insinuated his Opel among these columns, weaving in and out until he quickly disappeared from sight. Kuznetsov had left our atrád for the last time, I was the last man in our atrád to see him alive. After the war, I was asked very many times about this last meeting with Kuznetsov.

PART FIVE

Our "retreat" toward Lvov continued, and I proceeded with my unit, the support detachment of the command staff. Our unit had two full wagon-loads of arms. Once, in the middle of the night, as we were moving along a main road, our "Siberian," Kamishov, called to me, "Kohn, please, I'm having terrible cramps! I can't stand it! Take the reins while I run into that hut to relieve myself. I can't go on like this — my gut is being ripped apart!" I said, "Okay, Kamishov, but be quick about it." He said, "Thanks. I'll only take a few minutes, and I'll catch up with you." I went up on the wagon and took the reins. I had gone only 300 meters when a wheel broke and the wagon tilted over a bit. I continued, but it was a very heavy wagon. After another two kilometers I saw that I couldn't keep up with our unit, and Kamishov was nowhere in sight.

Things looked bad. There were German units in the vicinity who served as a rear guard, protecting the retreat of the main body of troops. Banderovets units were plentiful in that area, too. At first I thought I would leave the horses and wagon and run ahead as fast as I could. That way I might catch up with my unit and explain my problem to them. But then I reflected a bit and saw that I couldn't just abandon a wagon loaded with valuable arms.

The road had a soft shoulder. I drove the wagon onto it and then past it into a ditch. I camouflaged the wagon with branches from the forest, and I moved off five or six meters from the wagon and camouflaged myself. I hoped that my comrades would notice my absence or that Kamishov would catch up with them and tell them about me; they would then send somebody back for me.

I prepared my rifle and took out several grenades. If the worst happened I would fight till the last moment. I waited several hours like that, and the sky began to lighten. I heard talking from afar; when it's quiet in the forest you can hear any sound from some distance away. I listened very carefully. The snatches I heard weren't German, so the source of the sounds must be Banderovtsy. I put my finger on the trigger. The sounds came closer and closer, and then — I recognized our own people. I felt a sense of enormous relief, as if a lead weight had been lifted from my chest.

I learned something new about our atrád then. Whenever we moved, two platoons protected the move. One platoon served as a rear guard, moving ten or fifteen kilometers behind the main body of the atrád, and the other platoon served as a forward unit, moving ten or fifteen kilometers ahead of the main body. At that time, Lyonya Kyanov and his platoon were serving as our rear-guard unit, and it was their voices that I had heard.

When they came close to my position, I jumped out and explained my predicament to Kyanov. He told me to go on ahead until I saw a village on my left. I was to turn left in that village, and there I would find our atrád. I followed his orders and found our men. We all had a good laugh about the predicament I had found myself in as a result of Kamishov's unruly bowels. This episode could have had very different and tragic results, however.

When we moved to Galicia, we were told that our destination was an area near Lvov; then we would proceed to the Bug River, cross it, and move into Poland with the Germans.

The Germans, however, knew all about our atrád. They shrugged off the harassment they received from other atráds, but Medvedev's atrád had hurt them substantially, and they knew it. That close call I had due to Kamishov's bowels had taken place when we were about eighty kilometers from the Bug. Behind us a German division was retreating and blowing up all the bridges. Our reconnaissance discovered that a mighty German armored force was waiting for us at the Bug, so Moscow ordered us to turn back. On our way back, we had to wade across rivers and streams, which made the going very difficult. And we still had to use force to ram our way down certain roads and through many villages.

At this time, the exact condition of Krutikov's small advance group was reported to us. As I mentioned earlier, Krutikov's group was supposed to have set up a base camp for our atrád near Lvov to support Kuznetsov in his work, but they never made it to the designated area. They never, in fact, made it anywhere. They had been virtually eliminated.

As we retreated, we were followed for 150 kilometers by a German division. Another German division took up a blocking position in front of us, so we were caught in a squeeze. When the two divisions linked up on their flanks, they encircled us completely. The Germans had planned this trap very carefully, and they began to tighten the noose. All this took place near the village where I had replaced Kamishov on the broken wagon.

The Germans pushed us out of the hamlet into a nearby forest. We were saved from total annihilation by a near miracle. The battle lasted for two days. Our commander during this desperate struggle was Stekhov, who maintained constant radio contact with Moscow. At the end of the second day, we noticed that the Germans suddenly began to destroy their heavy equipment and burn their supplies. They had been on the verge of destroying us, and here they were committing military suicide! We saw raging fires and heard terrible explosions; we noticed German soldiers running around like madmen. What had happened was very simple: the Germans had surrounded us, but they, in turn, had been totally surrounded by the Red Army. The Red Army couldn't really throw all their might against the Germans because they knew that we — 1,500 men — were in the middle. Germans were destroying their equipment because they saw that the trappers had suddenly become the trapped. Towards the end of the second day of the battle, the Red Army punched a corridor through the trap around us. They led us out, and then they proceeded to smash the Germans completely. Two divisions were destroyed.

We were given a splendid welcome by the Red Army. I can't explain now how I felt then. This was the first time since 1941 that I was in really safe hands, but so much had happened since then. So many lives had been lost, so many good people were gone. . . . Almost nothing was left of my people in that area. They were all gone, and I had disappeared too. The young man who went into the woods around Trochenbrot-Ignatovka was no more.

Well, we were in safe hands, but what happened to Kuznetsov during this time? Kuznetsov knew that Krutikov's preparatory group was supposed to be in a certain area near Lvov, but when he arrived there the group was nowhere around. He then went into Lvov, where he was supposed to meet members of the anti-Nazi underground. He had been given a number of addresses. For several days, he checked them all, but the underground people weren't there; he searched high and low for them without success. Kuznetsov saw now that he would have to work on his own. He no longer had any contact with us, and he had failed to link up

[222]

with the Lvov local underground. He only had Belov and Kaminski now.

Kuznetsov's mission now was to eliminate as many of the German "big fish" as he could. The Germans called a special conference of senior German officers to be held in the Lvov Opera House. They were to be briefed about the military situation, and they were to receive the new orders. You needed a special ticket to enter the Opera House, but Kuznetsov managed to obtain one.

The Germans, however, were hot on the trail of the "German officer" who had assassinated so many of their senior officers. Valya Dovger had been caught, Stukalo had been captured and his wife killed, and Kulikovskaya (Vera Grebanovna's mother) had been hanged. Some others too from our atrád had been hanged. A Gestapo agent started to question Lydia Lisovskaya closely about Hauptmann Paul Siebert, so Lydia started to feel a bit hot under the collar. She wanted to get out of Rovno, but hundreds of thousands of Germans were crowding the trains, which were not moving properly anyway since we had blown up the railroad station. The Gestapo agent had come to like Lydia, so he used his influence to help her get from Rovno to Lvov. She decided to look for Kuznetsov, but she was really clueless as to his whereabouts. She set out to infiltrate the milieu of German officers, and she got to know one fairly senior officer well. For one of her dates with him, she was supposed to wait for him at the door of the Opera House. As she waited, she noticed Kuznetsov coming out. She was overjoyed, but she couldn't show it at all. She covertly set up a meeting with him for that evening, and they were soon working together against the German beasts, as in the Rovno days.

The main speaker at this Opera House conference was the Vice-Governor of Galicia, General Doctor Otto Bauer. Two days after the conference, Kuznetsov killed this satanic beast, and he also killed a very important German general, Schneider. As Schneider left his house for work at 8 A.M., Kuznetsov approached him and asked to see his documents; it was only a routine check, and all papers were to be examined. Kuznetsov was so sorry to disturb the esteemed General in this way, but he had his orders. The papers confirmed Schneider's identity, so Kuznetsov shot him, returned to his car, and sped away.

The Germans sent the bullets from the Lvov assassinations to their ballistics experts, who quickly discovered that the bullets came from the same revolver that had been used in the Rovno jobs. The Germans now knew certainly that one man was the cause of all their losses of senior German officers. The Gestapo therefore set a trap: all German officers had to be informed *personally*, by their commanding officers, that they were to wear a certain cape over their uniforms. Kuznetsov had no "commanding officer"; he was on his own, so he never heard about this order, and he went around without the cape. As he walked down a street, a major approached him. The dragnet had started. The major waited till Kuznetsov walked by an area full of Germans, and then he approached him and asked to see his papers. Kuznetsov took out his documents and the German saw that something was amiss. He said to Kuznetsov, "I must detain you for a few minutes. We must go to the military police commandant's office." Kuznetsov took out a special pass and said, "I'm on a top secret, special mission, and if you interfere . . ." However, the major was adamant and insisted, "I have my orders, and they mentioned no exceptions. I cannot disobey. Let's go."

So the major and Kuznetsov went to the city commandant's headquarters. Kuznetsov's car, driven by Belov, followed the two men at a safe distance and remained unnoticed. They went into the headquarters building, and the major reported to the German colonel who was serving as the commandant. He said, "Sir, I stopped this Hauptmann because he was not following the special order that came through yesterday." The major then went out and sat in the waiting room while Kuznetsov remained with the colonel. The colonel examined Kuznetsov's documents, and he too saw that something was wrong. He telephoned somewhere, and they seemed to be waiting for the call. The call was speedily routed through to an express number that had been established for a special purpose. As the colonel started to speak, Kuznetsov took out his silencer-equipped revolver and killed him. As he left the office, Kuznetsov told the major in the waiting room, "Ah, I don't envy you. You obstructed my urgent mission. The colonel asked me to tell you to come into his office in five minutes. He wants to see you, and there will be hell to pay for your stupidity!" Kuznetsov, at that point, saw that he had to get out of Lvov fast.

A great alarm swept through Lvov. All official personnel were placed on high alert. A street-by-street dragnet was begun. As Kuznetsov's car was leaving the city, a German roadblock loomed up. This was located twenty kilometers from Lvov, near a hamlet named Kurovichina. The roadblock was under the command of a German major, Kanter, who had some soldiers and a guard booth. An order had already gone out that the Lvov area was to be sealed 100 percent tight — nobody was to be allowed out. Kuznetsov's car was stopped at the roadblock, and it was soon surrounded by troops.

Major Kanter had already been warned, so he ordered Belov to drive the car over to the guard booth. He examined Kuznetsov's papers and asked for additional identification.

Kuznetsov saw that he would have to resort to force; pretending to reach into his pocket for more papers, he took out his revolver instead and shot Kanter. He shouted to Belov, "Let's get out of here — fast; step on it!" Kaminski had kept his submachine gun hidden in a ready position under some clothes. He started to spray the area of the guard booth as the car pulled away, and he killed eight German soldiers.

By the time the Germans recovered from their confusion, Kuznetsov's car was fifteen or twenty kilometers away. It was, however, being pursued. Kuznetsov, Kaminski, and Belov saw that there was no other way out, so they drove the car into the roadside trees and ran into the forest. The Gestapo soon found the car, but our men were already in the deep woods. They had no contact with our atrád or any friendly party at this point, and this lack of contact made matters desperate. With a contact, one man could do much. Without a contact, many men could do little. The Germans were chasing our three men, and the countryside was generally peopled by hostile, nationalist elements. Our men were between the devil and the deep blue sea.

Managing somehow to elude their pursuers, they wandered around the woods for several days before they finally decided to try to move in the direction of the advancing Red Army. As they moved through the forest, they ran into a large group of Jewish partisans led by Ehrlich. This group of "unofficial" partisans, operating in the Lvov area, consisted of 200 men. Ehrlich had no contact with anybody — he was on his own in those woods. When his men saw a German officer in the woods, they immediately opened fire. Kaminski managed to shout to them above the sound of the echoing gunfire, and the shooting quickly ceased. Ehrlich's men took our three men in, fed them, and refreshed them.

Kuznetsov asked Ehrlich and his men if they had any

knowledge at all of official partisans in that general area. They answered that they knew two official partisans who were recuperating, in hiding, nearby. Ehrlich's men used to help those two. So Kuznetsov asked to be led to them, and Ehrlich's men brought him to a point five kilometers away, where Kuznetsov found two men from Medvedev's atrád: Drozdov and Pristupa. Both were slowly recovering from typhus, and they were overjoyed to see Kuznetsov. They explained to him, "We were part of a group that was pushing on to the Lvov area. Our radio operator was killed, and we had to slug our way through every village and hamlet. The resistance to us was almost fanatical. We became sick so we were left here, but the rest of the group continued. Didn't you meet them in Lvov?" Kuznetsov explained how he found nobody except Lydia Lisovskaya in Lvov, and how he had had to leave in a great hurry. He told them about generals Bauer and Schneider, whom he had killed.

Drozdov suggested to Kuznetsov that he should remain with them till the Red Army advanced into that area. Ehrlich also suggested that Kuznetsov, Belov, and Kaminski should remain with the large Jewish group until the front approached. It was close by then. But Kuznetsov rejected these suggestions, and this rejection cost him his life. Kuznetsov wanted to push towards the front and cross into liberated territory. So, after saying their farewells to Ehrlich, Drozdov, and Pristupa, Kuznetsov and his two colleagues set out for the front.

Near the Brody road, at the halfway point between Rovno and Lvov, the three men saw a small house. They had been in the woods for a week since leaving Ehrlich's group, so they determined to go into the house to rest. It was early in the morning. Kuznetsov placed Belov in the front yard as a watch, and both he and Kaminsky went into the house. They sat down and asked the owner, who seemed friendly, for something to eat. Kuznetsov, as a precaution, had placed a large grenade under his hat, which he had put on the table.

Our three men didn't know that their luck had turned. By entering this house, they had stumbled upon a twenty-man Banderovtsy-type group, who were hiding; ten men were in the cellar, and ten were in the kitchen. As the owner of the house brought the food in, the kitchen door burst open, and ten heavily armed nationalists rushed in. One of their leaders shouted gleefully, "Ah, that's him — the Soviet bandit who is wanted so badly! They're searching high and low for him!" The Germans had offered 200 gold pieces as a reward for the capture of Kuznetsov. The nationalists told Kuznetsov to surrender; they intended to capture him alive.

Kuznetsov tried to negotiate with those Ukrainian nationalists. He told them how close the Red Army was; he was ready to guarantee their safety; he would vouch for them; the German cause was a lost cause. The nationalists were softening, because Kuznetsov was drumming some hard sense into their thick heads. However, just at the crucial moment, the ataman (commander-in-chief) of this nationalist group came in and said, "Ah, this is the guy we're looking for! Here's my 200 gold pieces!" Kuznetsov couldn't get over to his submachine gun, which was hanging on the wall, but the grenade was still under his hat. Kuznetsov saw that the ataman's arrival had sealed his fate, so he said, "Okay, I know when I'm licked. I'm going with you." He got up, knocked the oil lamp down so that the place became dark, lifted his hat, grabbed the grenade, and pulled the pin. As he pulled it, he shouted, "Look, dogs! This is how Soviet spies die!" He blew himself up and took seven or eight nationalists with him.

The owner of the house had tipped off the nationalists in

the cellar as to the number and whereabouts of Kuznetsov's companions. Belov, in the front yard, had been looking outwards with his back to the house, so they had moved in on him from the rear and, using a hammer, had given him a skull-crushing blow on the head. He died right there. When Kuznetsov blew himself up, Kaminski used the confusion to leap through the window. But he didn't get very far from the house, and he was killed in the yard.

What I have been telling you had to be painfully reconstructed long after the war. Kuznetsov's story, for a long time, stopped with Ehrlich and his men, and with Pristupa and Drozdov. They were the last to see him alive. Nobody knew what had happened to Kuznetsov and his two colleagues. I was questioned extensively about my last view of Kuznetsov, as his car joined the long columns of retreating Germans. Had Kuznetsov been killed or captured alive and taken to Germany?

Medvedev and Lukin learned from Drozdov and Pristupa that Kuznetsov had set out through the fields and woods alongside the Brody road. From these two partisans nothing more could be learned. After the Red Army took Lvov, Medvedev and Lukin examined all the German archives left unburned there. They saw that Kuznetsov had killed generals Bauer and Schneider, and a major named Kanter, who belonged to a German military police unit. Medvedev also saw, in the captured archives, that the OUN members (Organization of Ukrainian Nationalists, similar to the Banderovtsy but more closely linked with the Germans) had killed a terrible spy who went around as a German officer named Zilbert. That's the alias as it was written in those captured German archives. So Medvedev and Lukin finally found out what had happened to Kuznetsov. But the details about his end would remain a mystery for a long time.

[229]

After the war, there was a certain interest in this shadowy figure, Kuznetsov, alias Grachov, alias Paul Siebert, who had accomplished almost legendary feats. Kuznetsov's younger brother was an officer in the Soviet Army. I corresponded with him, and he wanted to know the details of the last time I had seen his brother. He even came from Sverdlovsk to discuss Kuznetsov with me and with many other former partisans. I met Kuznetsov's sister, too. One man, however, got to the bottom of the whole thing: Kolya Strutinsky. Strutinsky had worked closely with Kuznetsov for three years, and he just couldn't rest until he discovered the truth. After the war, he worked in Lvov as an MGB (Ministry of State Security) officer. He took the captured archives and documents, and for ten years he did intensive research. He followed up every possible lead, however farfetched; he interviewed every single surviving member of Ehrlich's Jewish group; he questioned everybody who was even remotely involved.

Masses of Banderovtsy from the Ukrainian villages and hamlets were in jail. Strutinsky questioned them carefully. By accident, he hit on the name of a nationalist, imprisoned in Siberia, who had been a member of the OUN group that had killed Kuznetsov; this nationalist was one of the twenty men in the house when Kuznetsov met his end. It took Strutinsky a dozen years to find the name of this man, and he had him brought back from Siberia. This nationalist told Strutinsky all about Kuznetsov's final moments.

A special commission of inquiry was formed and they took this nationalist back to the place where that house was located. He showed where the grenade exploded, where the others were killed. Of course, this nationalist "explained" his own role in the matter: he had thought that Kuznetsov was a German. He wore a German uniform, didn't he? So this nationalist tried to show that he was only trying to do his patriotic duty by capturing a German officer. He was, of course, lying through his teeth, but he wasn't treated roughly by the commission — he was, after all, their primary source of information. Without him, the whole investigation would be up against a stone wall. Following the nationalist's directions, the commission found Kaminski's skeleton, which was buried only ten meters from the house. Kuznetsov's grave was also found. Kuznetsov had a unique physical characteristic — a double tooth. The skull in the shallow grave also had such a double tooth. In the grave they found the remnants of a letter, and this letter was one that had been written to Kuznetsov.

In October of 1959, Moscow sent a renowned expert in forensic medicine to Lvov: Dr. M. M. Gerassimov, who came from the most respected Moscow institute. He was joined by another expert, V. Djelengurov, from Lvov. They were given a skull that had been shattered in fifteen places, and they were told to match it with one of many photos of faces placed before them. After much study and measurement, they matched the skull with the photo of a certain man's face. That face was Kuznetsov's.

Kuznetsov was buried in Lvov with full military honors in 1959. His funeral procession was the longest that had ever been seen in Lvov. It stretched for blocks and blocks, and people crowded the streets and balconies to get a glimpse of the coffin carrying the last remains of this one man who had done so much against the Nazi vampires.

So, in 1959, Kuznetsov was laid to rest by the Red Army that he had tried so hard to reach on those fateful days of 1944. As I mentioned before, our atrád was led out of a gigantic German trap by the Red Army. After we spent some time with the Red Army, Moscow ordered us to move to liberated Tsuman for rest and recuperation. We were billeted in houses, and we remained there for three weeks. There were many Banderovtsy in nearby hamlets and in the surrounding forests, and we fought them often. Now we were in the towns and villages, and they were in the woods. Two hundred fifty of our men were detached from the atrád and given other functions. Some became policemen, because a basis for the future civilian life in the area was being established; others joined the NKVD or regular army. Medvedev was recalled to Moscow, and Stekhov was sent to Drohobych. Lukin took over command of our atrád.

After another week or ten days, another 200 men were detached from the atrád and given other assignments. One night, we were woken up and informed that a major Banderovtsy supply base had been discovered in a hamlet thirty kilometers from Tsuman. We moved out under Malik's command, surrounded the hamlet, and found out where the supplies were hidden. There were hundreds of tons of supplies hidden there, and it took us five or six days to move it out. We were then ordered back to Tsuman.

On our way back, I was on horseback. We moved slowly all night, and the next day we approached Derazhno, a village that had served as the headquarters of the Banderovets high command in 1942 and 1943. When we were five or six kilometers from Derazhno, a fellow partisan who was on foot came over to me. He was an Asiatic from one of the Soviet Eastern Republics. He said, "Kohn, please, I'm dead tired — let me get on the horse." I told him to wait; we were only five or six kilometers from our next stop, and there he would rest. He went away, but after ten minutes he returned. He was virtually begging, "Kohn, I can't walk anymore. Please!" I couldn't say no, so I got off the horse and said, "Okay, here's the horse. As soon as we come to the next hamlet, give it back to me."

[232]

He was short and stocky, but he leaped up on the horse with one bound. I moved over to the edge of the forest, and I proceeded on foot. I hadn't gone very far when I heard a loud explosion. I ran over to the horse, but it was no longer there. Pieces of it were scattered everywhere. The horse had stepped on a mine, and the shrapnel had done its bloody work. I was the first on the scene, and then Valya Semyonov ran over. He asked me, "How did this fellow happen to be on that horse? You were in that saddle five minutes ago." I told Valya what had happened. The Asiatic partisan was in very bad shape. We called for the return of one of our wagons, which was up the road by now; we put the partisan on it, and Valya told me to get on too. I told him that I couldn't — my nerves were shot.

We took our partisan comrade into the hamlet. Troops from the Red Army were there, and a doctor examined him. The doctor simply shrugged and said that nothing could be done — the man would be dead within an hour. We waited until he died, and we buried him in that hamlet, fifteen kilometers from Tsuman. When we moved off, Valya came over to me and said, "Pull yourself together, Kohn! It wasn't your fault; it was his destiny. Now I can see why you were nicknamed the 'Vezuche,' the lucky one!"

We returned to Tsuman and spent another three weeks there. Lukin put all our atrád's files in order for Moscow. One day we received a new group of atrád commanders from Moscow. Colonel Ivanov became the commander, and his associate, who replaced Lukin, was Major Zakharov. Ivanov questioned every company commander, and Zakharov called every partisan into his office and interrogated each separately. Three hundred men were detached from our atrád and sent away. Only 700 were left now. After several days, another 250 were detached, so we were left with

450 men. I was among these 450 men. We rested for another week, and then we were given shining new weapons. We had the latest automatic weapons now; even the lowest-ranking helper or driver was magnificently equipped. And then our new orders came through — we were to infiltrate the German lines and continue our work behind their lines.

So we prepared to cross the front into German-occupied territory. Our 450 men left Tsuman on the road to Carpathia; there we would lunge over the front into German-occupied territory. We stopped in the villages now, not in the forests around them as we had done in the old days. We saw that it would be very hard to go through Carpathia with our heavy wagons, so we discarded the wagons and lashed our ammunition and equipment to the horses' backs. We surely wouldn't have been able to go through that mountainous country with our heavy wagons; we even had to teach the horses how to proceed on those mountainous cliffside trails. Sometimes one fell to its death; they weren't used to that kind of thing.

We were near the front very many times. When we would come to the front, ready to cross, the front would advance another twenty kilometers and we'd have to try again. And this pattern was repeated many times. Thinking it over now, I wonder why we spent so much time wandering around near the front like that; we could have crossed the front lines on any one of many occasions. My own idea is that Colonel Ivanov was not eager to cross the German lines; it certainly seemed like that. Ivanov's leadership was not Medvedev's; Medvedev would try to get into battle on every occasion; Medvedev looked for a fight and sought to engage the enemy. Ivanov was not like that. Even among our rank-and-file partisans there was a certain distrust of Ivanov's leadership. Morale was very low. Of course, we only whispered our feelings to each other or hinted at them. We asked: What are we waiting for? Why all these pauses? The Red Army moves farther every time we hesitate. Ivanov had direct contact with the Red Army — he knew when it would advance or stand still. He had exact knowledge of their movements. So why were we always being left behind?

Many times, when we woke up in the morning, we would find two or three empty places in our ranks. The missing men hadn't deserted — they had simply left us to join the nearest Red Army unit in the vicinity. The partisans wanted to make an end of the war; this was their aim. They were tired of the war, and they wanted to participate in bringing it to a quick end. And with Ivanov we weren't participating at all. We felt that something was amiss. We had become the fifth leg of the dog.

I once had a chance to leave myself. We were in a certain village, and a Soviet Air Force lieutenant-colonel came to see me; I don't know where he had heard about me. Oresov was now head of the command support group, in which I still served. He told me that a lieutenant-colonel wanted to see me, and when I reported to him, he asked, "Are you the watchmaker?" I answered, "Yes." He said, "Our airfield is close by. We need a man with watchmaking skills to repair our instruments and gauges. We're short of technical personnel." I answered, "I can't. It's almost four and a half years that I've been with the partisans. We're near the end of the war. How could I abandon them now?" He said to me, "What's the diffierence? You're helping defeat the Germans if you're with us just as much as if you remain a partisan. We're all participating in smashing the rotten Germans. You're of much greater value to us than you can ever be here. You have special skills — we need them." Despite the sense of his argument, I answered, "I simply can't leave." He also proposed to give me a field commission as a junior officer.

At that time, I was very good friends with Mikhail Kutavoy. (He died in a car crash after the war; until his death we were closer than brothers.) I went to ask Mikhail's advice. He looked at me and said, "Naum, I can't advise you now — it's up to you." But in his eyes I could see that he was ready to understand if I should decide to join the colonel.

Sometime later, I said to Mikhail, "I would consider the colonel's proposition if Major Zakharov or Colonel Ivanov would give me official permission to leave." Mikhail said, "Okay, I'll go see them." He returned in an hour, shaking his head. "They refuse to agree, but Naum, follow my advice — do it! Join the Soviet Air Force! It's not a crime you're committing."

That evening, the Colonel came again and said to me, "Tomorrow morning we're pulling out of this area. There's an intersection down the road. At six A.M., my car will be stopped there, waiting for you."

I didn't answer. Nor did I sleep most of that night. At 6 A.M., I went out and walked over to a hill overlooking that intersection; I heard the idling motor of a car, quietly chugging away. The car waited there for an hour. But I just couldn't go. I had gone through practically the whole war — four and a half years — with the partisans. I had lived through so much bad and so much good with them. We had become welded together closer than brothers. How could I pick up and go? And if I went, how could I live with my conscience? I never joined that car, and it left without me.

Fifty men from Ivanov's original group accompanied him when he took over leadership of Medvedev's atrád. Among these fifty men, three were Germans; two actually came from Germany (one named Karol), and the other was a Volga

[236]

German from the Soviet Union. I got to know those three Germans well when we were billeted in Tsuman. I knew some German — Sieradz was near the Polish-German border, and I used to hear my father speak German often. The three Germans lived in separate quarters from us, but we ate together, and I used to talk to them often. They had a special mission, but I didn't know what it was. I got along well with them, especially with Karol, who was a very friendly fellow. During the Spanish Civil War, Karol and his friend had fought with the communists against Franco, and when Franco won they made their way to a British colony. In 1942, when Britain and the Soviet Union became allies, they asked, as communists, to be sent to the Soviet Union.

One day, Major Zakharov called on me, and asked me, "Kohn, you were born in Poland, weren't you?" When I said, "Yes," he asked, "What place in Poland?" I said, "Sieradz, in western Poland, about sixty kilometers from Lodz." Zakharov continued, "How would you feel about being dropped by parachute with a small group into that area?" To tell you the truth, I was taken aback, but in my heart I was very happy. I know it sounds stupid now, but I thought then that I would be closer to home where I knew the forests and streams. I didn't know then that my family was dead. I had a dim idea of getting into Sieradz and rescuing my family. Although I had fought the Nazis for four and a half years, I couldn't imagine the extent of the Holocaust. I had heard about concentration camps; I had listened carefully to the rumors that came to us in the forest. I knew about the mass graves of slaughtered Jews all over the Ukraine, but the dimensions of the death factories surpassed my imagination. The Germans had been retreating since Stalingrad; surely, they wouldn't divert much-needed manpower, supplies, and transportation to kill millions of civilians. It didn't make sense! Anyway, in my heart of hearts I didn't want to believe the worst, and that's why I kept my illusions.

A short time after my conversation with Zakharov, several high officers came from Moscow. Ivanov's atrád was dismantled, and small groups were formed. I was called in twice for interviews, and I was finally placed with the Germans (Karol and the other two) in one group. The radio operator Bezugly was also in our group, which was supposed to number twelve to sixteen men. I was eager for this parachute jump. It meant something to me: besides rescuing my family, on my home ground I would settle up with the Germans for what they had done to innocent Jews. This would be personal revenge! We were supposed to be transported to Lvov, where we would be trained to jump with parachutes. It would take some time to teach us. We were all packed ready to move out, when, at the last moment, I was ordered, with one other man, to remain behind while the rest of the group left. Why we weren't taken is a mystery to me to this very day. We just weren't taken.

We were in Kurovichi, not far from Lvov, and by now almost everybody had left. Ivanov was still with us but Zakharov had left. Only twenty or twenty-five men remained from the whole atrád. Ivanov assembled us and told us that we were going to Lvov, and from there on to Kiev, where he would transfer us to the Kiev MGB. He himself was traveling on to Moscow.

It took us about a day to get to Lvov. We took our best horses with us. There were no railroad passenger cars in that war-ravaged area, so we used cattle cars. They were quite clean, however. The distance from Lvov to Kiev is about 580 kilometers, and it took us a full five days to cover the distance. The railroad tracks were still in very bad shape.

We finally arrived in Kiev, and a reception committee was

waiting for us at the station. Cars and trucks were lined up, and we were given a very warm welcome. At the station, a Major Sevelov gave a speech about who we were and what we had accomplished. A crowd of civilians quickly grew around us; they had never seen partisans before. We carried our weapons proudly, and we were a crusty lot — we must have given those civilians quite an eyeful!

We were brought into Kiev and received fraternally, with great warmth. From Kiev, we were sent thirty kilometers to an MGB farm for five or six weeks of rest and recuperation. They gave us two cabins there and assigned a special cook to us, who was ordered to cook whatever we wanted. This was quite something when you consider that strict food rationing was still in force then.

After my stay at the farm ended, I was called into MGB headquarters in Kiev, and they explained to me that I couldn't return home because Warsaw was still occupied by the Germans. They suggested that I work as a watchmaker in OXO — a big government shop where various skilled tradesmen worked. Kuznetsov's private tailor in our atrád, Drachman, worked there too. The Germans used to marvel at the fit and quality of Kuznetsov's uniforms, which had been painstakingly sewn in the forest by Drachman. I accepted the MGB offer of work, and I was soon back at a worktable repairing watches and clocks.

My partisan career, which had brought me from the forests of Trochenbrot-Ignatovka to Kiev, was over.

POSTSCRIPT

I had been working for a month or so in the large OXO shop when a security guard who was normally stationed at our shop's front door came over to my area of the shop and asked, "Who around here is named Kohn?" I was sitting at a bench, working, and I answered, "I'm Kohn." The guard said, "A relative has come to see you. He says he's your brother." I jumped up! I soon had to sit down because I became quite dizzy. I asked, "Where? Who?" The guard said, "He's standing at the entrance. Go out and see him." I ran over to the main entrance, and there standing quietly, was Mikhail Kutavoy, my partisan brother-in-arms. Mikhail had been my close friend during those years in the forest, and his warm sympathy and friendship had helped keep me on an even keel when my spirits were low.

Well, we embraced. He had tears in his eyes. I asked him, "Where are you coming from?" He answered, "I've come from Lvov specially to see you." I asked, "How did you know where I was working?" He told me, "In Lvov I was told that you were in Kiev. I used to work in Kiev as an engineer for the railroad, so I had friends here who located you for me." Mikhail had a university degree in engineering, and now he was working in Lvov as a chief engineer in charge of repairing steam engines.

The guard looked at us embracing; he saw the joy that suffused us both, so he went off to the supervisor and said that Kohn's brother had found him. Everybody in my shop area rejoiced with me. I went to my foreman, the same Major Sevelov who had made a speech greeting us in the Kiev railway station. I wanted to explain the situation to him, but he cut me off. He said, "I know, I know, your brother came. Okay, Kohn, how much time off do you want? Three days, four days — you can have as much time off as you want!" I said. "He's not my brother. We were partisans side-by-side for a long time. He's like a brother to me — maybe even more!" Sevelov said he understood. He soon filled out a special pass for me and my guest allowing us to go into restaurants for lunch. At that time food was still in *extremely* short supply; eating lunch altogether was a rare treat; eating lunch in a restaurant was a great privilege.

I took Mikhail to my room, where I had some food. I had a hot plate in the room. I asked Mikhail when he had left Lvov, and he told me, "I've been traveling for five days to see you." I said, "Mikhail, wash up, take a rest. Meanwhile, I'll go down to the market to buy something, and we'll have a meal." He said, "Okay, I am a bit sweaty and grimy." I ran downstairs and went down the street to the market, where I bought a can of American Lend-Lease jam, a bread, and a few eggs. I ran back, and I saw that Mikhail was dozing.

While he slept, I set the table. I always kept in my room five or six bottles of vodka. As I told you, before the war I never drank; nor did I drink during the war, except for that unfortunate incident with the spiritus when I was serving in the demolition squad of Medvedev's atrád. That drink had put me in the hospital.

I took two glasses, poured Mikhail a drink and one for me, and said, "Mikhail, my friend, my brother, I drink a toast in honor of your visit!" We drank to our old comrades who had fallen in battle; we drank to the atrád; we drank to the victory over the Germans. Then I saw Mikhail's eyes turn red with

[244]

anger. He jumped up and gave me an enormous whack right across the face. I was younger (24) and healthier than he was then, but my face was smarting from the blow he had just given me. He was wearing a Russian-type jacket, so I grabbed him by the lapels. He burst out, "I don't want to see you any more!" And he ran out of my room and down to the street. I couldn't understand his behavior. I ran after him and caught him at the downstairs door. "Mikhail, what happened? What did I do? How did I offend you? If I'm guilty I'll admit it, but what in hell did I do?" He didn't want to talk to me. I said, "Okay talk or don't talk. But I'm just asking you: you've traveled five days. Come back up. Just tell me why you feel offended, what I did to you, and why you hit me!"

He went back up, and when he regained his composure he said to me, "Listen, Naum, after we parted I went around for a month looking for my wife and son. I finally found them and brought them to Lvov. I told them all about you, how you were the soul of decency and honesty, how you had fought alone with your Jewish group against the murderers, how we both kept each other's morale high! I spent a long time looking for you. You told me that you were to be dropped in Poland, so I inquired there. When I located you in Kiev, my joy was great! I went to my superiors, and I told them that I *had* to have a lengthy leave from my job because I *had* to see you. You know the condition of the engines now — most of them are unusable and they're crying for immediate repairs. But I was adamant, and my superiors gave me the time off that I had requested. So I came to Kiev and found my Naum. And who do I see? A God-damn drunk, that's who! I told everybody about you, and now a drunk stands before me."

I said, "Look, Mikhail." I took out many letters and put them down before him. I wrote home to Sieradz many times.

[245]

I wrote to my neighbors. I wrote to the City Hall. I wrote to the police. The replies all said the same thing: 'All the members of your family were killed.' Mikhail, I am alone in the world. When I received those letters, I asked myself: Why did I remain alive? Why did I survive? Why did my family leave me alone like that? And I started to drink. Every day I drank; a couple of glasses at first, then a bit more as the empty days wore on. When I drank, I used to feel that they were all alive, with me, near me. Many times I used to return to my room and start to cry. I saw one fellow-worker going with a brother, another with a sister, but I was like a lost sheep. The flock had gone in one direction and I had gone off in another direction, and I was lost. I used to cry like a lost sheep that bleats in its panic and solitude, all alone. Look at my hair, Mikhail!" I have all of my hair to this very day, but it is pure white. In prewar days and during my service with the partisans, it was jet black. However, in the months after the war, when letter after letter came from Poland telling me to abandon all hope, I turned white. I was not yet 25, but I was all white.

Mikhail listened very carefully. Then he said to me, "Today it's a couple of glasses, tomorrow it'll be three and four glasses, and after a few years there'll be nothing left of you." I asked, "Mikhail, what do you want of me?" He said, "If you want to remain my friend and brother, take two small glasses and fill them — one drink for you and one drink for me. Then I want you to take your whole collection of bottles and smash each bottle before my eyes, and give me your word that you'll never drink again." I said, "Mikhail, these bottles cost me so much! A whole collection! Let me finish them off; then I'll stop drinking." His reply to my suggestion was swift and straightforward: "Ah, if that's what you want, then I'll leave now." His attitude made an extremely strong impression on me. I saw that when I turned to the bottles and started to smash them, tears ran from Mikhail's eyes. Those weren't an actor's tears; they were real, coming from the heart. I smashed every single one of my precious bottles.

Mikhail enjoyed the rest of his visit with me. I told him that I would come to Lvov to see his wife and son, and we spent much time reminiscing about old times and looking forward to better times. However, my friend and brother Mikhail was killed in a car accident several years later. I feel his loss every day.

Since that bottle-smashing day in my second-floor room, I have almost never had a drink.

* * *

In 1948, after I had moved from Kiev to Rovno, I learned that one of my cousins had survived and was living in Minsk (today she lives in New York). I sent her a telegram. Her father and my mother were brother and sister, and my mother's maiden name was Gliksman, so I sent the telegram to Gliksman. It took some time to get to her because her married name was Slobodskaya, but when it did, I got an answer that I should visit her immediately — she had to tell me something. She couldn't come to see me because she was in her last months of pregnancy. Shortly thereafter, I traveled to Minsk to see her.

Our reunion was very joyful — it's hard to explain the mixture of tears and joy. She fell apart completely; for three or four hours she was uncontrollable. We were sobbing, and our bodies were shaking. As for myself, I couldn't say one word — I was struck speechless. The next day we regained our composure, and we spoke non-stop for hours on end. She told me that her sister Dobcha was living in Belgium, and then she gave me her news: "Nahum, one of your brothers is alive." I jumped up: "Who?" A shiver ran through my body;

my skin was covered with goose pimples. She said, "I don't know exactly, but it sounded like Felix." (At home we had called him Fyvel.) She had been told that one of Tseeryl's sons (my mother was Tseeryl) was alive. I said, "Tell me exactly — what were Dobcha's words?" She repeated them for me five and ten times, and we soon ran to the post office to telephone Belgium. The connections were bad — we couldn't get through. I sent a telegram that I was alive and gave my address in Rovno. Could she please send me my brother's address immediately. I remained in Minsk for five or six days, and then I returned to Rovno.

After I had been back in Rovno for three weeks, I received a telegram from Israel, from my brother. He had been wounded in the War of Independence; he had been in the armored corps, and the telegram to me had been sent from a hospital. I answered him immediately by telegram, and from that time on we were in touch with each other.

The years passed, and I worked at my trade in Rovno. My *shtetl*, Sieradz, was always in my mind and heart, however. No day went by without a thought of those Sieradz streets and houses where I grew up. I had had a friend in Sieradz, a Polish Christian girl, Zosha, who lived in one of the houses fronting on our courtyard. She was always in my parents' home and was a good friend of us all; she was practically a member of our family. She was about a year older than I, and we had grown up together. I had always figured, in my blackest moments in the forest, that Zosha would protect my family. Zosha would watch over my relatives like a mother hen guarding its own. Many times in the woods I almost whispered her name aloud: Zosha, Zosha, the protector of my family, my source of hope.

One day I said to myself: I *must* go back to Sieradz, at least to find the grave of my own brothers, sisters, and parents, to stand there for several minutes and say a quiet Kaddish for their souls. Then I would know my relatives' last resting place; perhaps this knowledge would give me some peace. So, in 1964, I wrote my brother in Canada (where he was living then) and told him that I was going to Sieradz on a certain date. I received an answer from him asking me for my exact itinerary; he would try to travel to Poland to meet me.

My cousin Simcha was living in a Polish town, Dzierżoniów (formerly a German town, now under Polish sovereignty), and he sent me a visa for travel to Poland. You may remember that, after I had been living in Trochenbrot for four or five months, my cousin Simcha felt that we should retreat deeper into Russia, and he left. He later joined the Red Army and fought during the siege of Leningrad, where he was severely wounded. After his recovery, he was wounded again outside of Riga.

In 1964, I traveled to Poland with my daughter Helena, who was 12. In Dzierzoniow I said to Simcha, "Simcha, you remember Zosha?" He answered, "Of course, I remember her very well." Simcha knew Sieradz well because he had lived in our house for three years. I said, "You know, I think she must have behaved magnificently to my family. She'll tell me everything! I'll take the bus to Sieradz tomorrow; I can't wait to speak to her!" It was a trip of 600–700 kilometers, and Simcha insisited on accompanying me.

I had boarded that bus with one idea: to see Zosha. The minute I left the bus in Sieradz, I was overcome by one strong feeling: *I didn't want to see Zosha!* We went into the local hotel, and one of the hotel-keepers, an old woman, reacted immediately when she saw my name. There had been only three Kohns in Sieradz: a ritual slaughterer (a *shoychet*), my family, and one other. So when she saw Kohn on the register of the hotel she started to cry. I had planned to remain in Sieradz for two weeks, so I prepaid the hotel bill for the full two weeks.

It was early evening when we arrived. My daughter said, "Come, daddy, let's go see Zosha." I said, "No." "Why?" she asked. I answered, "I don't know, but we're not going anywhere now." It was early, and we could have gone out for two or three hours, but I just could not — it was as if I had suddenly become paralyzed.

The next day we went out on the street and started to walk straight to my parents' house, which was located downtown near a small square surrounded by three-storey houses. My hotel wasn't far from this square, and the third house on one of these streets, Zamkova, was my parents' home. I was walking slowly with my daughter, while Simcha walked on rapidly ahead. My daughter and I were still in the square; we hadn't yet reached the beginning of Zamkova Street when Simcha came running back to us and said, "Nahum, your house is no longer standing." I went to look. Ours had been a three-storey house; I now saw a new, two-storey building, a cultural club, standing on the site. I remained standing in front of this strange building; I couldn't go into the front yard.

Poles went by, and they recognized that Simcha was Jewish. They asked who we were and Simcha told them, "Kohn's son." One knew my father; another said she knew my sister well. I didn't want to say one word to anyone, however. We started to walk back to the hotel, but my daughter was hungry, so I told Simcha to go into a store and buy a bread and some milk. I sat down on a park bench, and, as I was sitting, an old man, a Polish Christian, sat down on the bench near me. He asked, "Are you of Mosaic ancestry?" I answered, "Yes. My name is Kohn." "Ah, Kohn," he said, "Zosha lives close-by. Here's her address." I said, "No — I don't want to see her." He tried to tell me the address but I cut him off and repeated, "No — I definitely don't want to see her. Please — leave me alone!"

All the years I had been drawn to Sieradz to speak to Zosha; it was as if a magnet had been pulling me back. And now I didn't want to see her. The old man was stubborn. He said, "She's living over there. She'll be very glad to see you." I asked, "Where do you live?" He said, "Over there, across the way." I said: "That's Dr. Kempinski's house." He was taken aback, but he quickly blurted out, "Yes, but I bought it before the war." I knew quite well that Kempinski had been dragged out of that house and killed during the war.

While I was sitting with that Pole, he pointed out a passing man to me, a Pole. He said, "That man is Glovatzki." Glovatzki had been a friendly competitor of my father. I stood up, went over to him, and stopped him. "Excuse me," I said. He stopped. "I'm Kohn," I said. He exclaimed, "You're Kohn? You became so white?" He thought that I was my father. I said, "No, I'm not the father, I'm one of the sons." Glovatzki invited me to stay at his house; that was decent of him. I explained to him that I was staying at the hotel, and then I asked him, "Perhaps you have a photo of my family, a memento, a souvenir? Perhaps you can tell me something of my folks — where they died, how they died?" He told me, "They took them to a nearby hamlet under the guise of transporting them for labor, but they put them in trucks, and while the trucks were moving they were gassed to death by the trucks' own exhaust systems. The trucks kept going, and they were buried somewhere in the forest. Nobody knows the exact location."

We returned to the hotel and I told my daughter and Simcha, "We're packing our valises *now* and leaving. I don't

[251]

want to stay here another minute. I don't want to see anything more here." They started to beg me, to implore me. They mentioned the distance we had traveled, the discomfort we had endured to get to Sieradz, the fact that we had prepaid our hotel bill, and so on. I answered, "Nothing will change my mind! Pack! Pack now!"

That same evening we left Sieradz and traveled back to Dzierzoniow. My cousin, Dr. Shtulman, was living in Lodz; he had wanted to see me very badly, so I went to visit him. While I was in Lodz, I received a telephone call from Simcha telling me that he had received a telegram from Canada informing him that my brother was coming. I returned to Dzierżoniów and waited.

One morning, I was alone in Simcha's house. Helena was playing outside. There was a knock at the front door, so I opened it. A man, one head taller than I was, was standing there with two valises at his feet. He said, "Nahum?" I blurted out, "Felix?" He said, "Yes." We embraced, but we were both speechless. He came in, and we put the two valises down. We sat for twenty minutes, paralyzed and speechless.

Simcha's wife Olga came in, and I said, "Olga, this is my brother." I introduced my daughter to Felix, and they embraced and spoke a bit. But Felix and I couldn't say one word to each other. We sat almost two hours like that, unable to talk to each other. Then Felix said to me, "I saw a park near here, didn't I? Do you know how to go there?" I said, "Yes." He said, "Let's go to the park." I wanted him to take a rest. He had come a long way." But he insisted, "I want to go to the park." I agreed, and we went out. Helena, who was playing out front, wanted to accompany us, but I told her to continue her games in the front yard.

We walked over to the park and didn't say one word to each other. He looked at me, and I looked at him. Our voices seemed to have deserted us. We came into the park, picked an isolated bench, and sat down. For half an hour we sat, speechless. Then I managed to say several words to him. All of a sudden, tears poured out of his eyes like a fountain. This lasted for half an hour, but I had no sooner calmed him down when I myself started to cry, uncontrollably, spasmodically. Now it was his turn to calm me down, and that took another forty minutes or so. We walked over to a fountain and washed our faces to hide the traces of the tears. We sat for ten more minutes in the park, and said a few words to each other. Out of twelve brothers and sisters, only the two of us were left, and the rest — gone with the wind.

On our return to Simcha's house, I was more composed, and I told Felix about my visit to Sieradz a short time before his arrival. Felix had been at home until well into 1942, when he was shipped off to a concentration camp, and he had seen a great deal of Sieradz under the German heel. I had left in the fall of 1939, so I asked him, "Who tried to help our family? We had so many Gentile friends in our town!" I found out how Berger, the German, had saved my father from the Warsaw ghetto and had been shot for this noble deed. I didn't mention Zosha to my brother. He brought up her name, and he told me all about her: how she systematically exploited my family, how she squeezed them out of their last possessions, how she terrorized them, how she threw my sister Paula and her two babies out on the street into the Germans' hands. Zosha first took over half the house, then three-quarters of the house, then all of it. She was one of the worst — she sucked the blood from my defenseless relatives. She oppressed them every minute of every day.

My head was exploding when I heard this litany of evil. My brother was a living eyewitness to the hell Zosha had imposed on my helpless family. Through all of the years I had lived with an illusion that somewhere, somehow, my relatives' suffering was mitigated by the efforts of our old family friend Zosha, who had been practically a member of our family. That illusion was finally stripped from me too, as so many others had been before.

* * *

Over 100,000 people (mostly prisoners of war) were killed by the Germans in Rovno. There are three large mass graves of murdered Jews on the Kiev Road, five kilometers from Rovno, in an area called Sosnovka. One mass grave contains 18,000 bodies, another contains 20,000 bodies, and a smaller one contains the remains of 5,000 children whose lives were cut short by the German butchers and their helpers.

These three mounds, overgrown and unmarked, became the target of treasure hunters after the war, who dug into them to find gold teeth. The Rovno dead Jews weren't even allowed to rest in peace after their deaths. Around 1950, two Latvians were caught digging in the grave mounds, looking for "treasure." They had been members of the original Nazi execution squad that had massacred the defenseless Jews. The two Latvians were caught and tried. From time to time, I heard about other cases where those pathetic mounds were desecrated.

After many protests, a low (two-foot-high) fence was erected around each mound, and a nondescript plaque was placed there. The plaque said: "Here Lie Soviet Citizens, Victims of Fascism." The remaining Jews of Rovno have, many times, asked that a suitable monument be erected on this tragic site, *a monument to Jews*. This request has been ignored. The authorities did erect an imposing monument to the victims of fascism. It was built at the other end of the town, as far as possible from the Jewish mass graves. This official monument is at the beginning of Belaya Street. The Jewish graves remain ignored and forgotten. In Lvov, the site of the Jewish mass graves has been turned into a soccer field.

I went into the woods that day, long ago, to fight for decency and justice, and I played my role, however small, in the defeat of the Nazi monsters who had condemned my people to death. They may build soccer fields over the bones of my brothers and sisters; the Jewish mass graves of Rovno may be ignored; but what I did can never be undone!